LONDON

E
62

KEN GLAZIER

Capital Transport

INTRODUCTION

This is one of a series of handbooks, each of which contains a complete list of all buses and coaches owned by London Transport during a period of four or five years, together with a brief description and history of each type covered. Vehicles which either joined or left the fleet during the period under review are listed with an additional column showing the dates on which they were formally taken into or removed from stock. These refer to the dates on which ownership changed and, in the case of buses taken out of stock, do not necessarily coincide with the day on which a vehicle left London Transport's hands physically. Vehicles sold for scrap were often dispatched to the breaker's yard before the paperwork was completed and some vehicles were stored by London Transport for a time after being sold to other operators. Where a body was scrapped before the chassis, the date on which the chassis was scrapped is deemed to be the date the complete vehicle was written off.

For the years after 1942 dates 'into stock' for all but experimental buses refer to the day on which the completed vehicle was received from the body builder. The chassis will have been owned for some time before this, however, as the normal procedure was for chassis to be delivered formally to London Transport, either physically or as a book transaction, before being sent for bodying.

The present volume covers the period from 1st January 1955 to 31st December 1962, a relatively quiet period so far as movements into and out of the fleet were concerned. Most of the Routemasters delivered did not replace motor buses, nearly all withdrawals during the five years being in response to reductions in service levels which began to be applied in earnest from 1955 onwards. These first cuts led to the premature withdrawal of the early post-war STD and STL types, the 2RT2s, the non-standard Craven bodied RTs and some of the Weymann bodied post-war Ts and TDs; but the prolonged strike by busworkers in 1958 prompted the even more premature sale of substantial numbers of standard post-war RTs and RTLs, as well as the remaining 14T12s and 1TD1s and some Mann Egerton Ts and TDs.

These books would not have been possible without the generous help of Dr Andrew Gilks, from whose private collection the bulk of the information concerning dates has been derived. Others who have given assistance include Ken Blacker, Lawrie Bowles and Reg Westgate who have helped to fill the various gaps, and Les Stitson who has worked hard on checking the accuracy of the basic data and taken a leading part in preparing the text for production. Thanks are also due to Brian Bunker, John Gent, Malcolm Papes and Dave Ruddom for allowing me to raid their photographic collections for illustrations and to the photographers, who are acknowledged separately in the body of the book, for permitting the use of their work.

First published 1999
ISBN 185414 211 9
© Capital Transport Publishing, Harrow Weald, Middlesex

CONTENTS

Title page
RT 310 turns into Oxford Street in 1960. *Alan B. Cross*

Front cover
RM 2 during its brief spell in green livery, pictured at Tattenham Corner.
A painting by Barry Pearce

The last Weymann bodied 18STL20s in service were those allocated to Hertford for route 327 on which there was a bridge with a weight restriction. Before being replaced by 2RT2s in June 1955 they were often to be found on Hertford's other double-deck routes. STL 2685 is at Havers Lane, Bishops Stortford, on route 350A. John C. Gillham

STL

The STL was first introduced by Thomas Tilling Ltd and the London General Omnibus Company in 1932 to take advantage of new Regulations which increased the maximum length of double-deckers from 25ft to 26ft. The developed design became London Transport's standard double-decker between 1933 and 1939. All were built on the AEC Regent 661 or 0661 chassis and from 1934 onwards the standard specification was for oil engine and preselective gearbox. In 1942 London Transport received thirty-four 'unfrozen' Regent chassis for which twenty lowbridge and fourteen highbridge austerity bodies were built at Chiswick. All of the lowbridge bodies and many of the highbridge version were fitted to standard chassis and most of the new chassis received bodies of various pre-war types from the works float. In 1946 a further twenty chassis of the post-war standard AEC design were purchased and these were fitted with Weymann's first post-war style of proprietary bodywork.

Use of unfrozen STLs as trainers and staff buses ceased in June 1955 but many remained in stock unused for another three years. Like all Aldenham staff buses STL 2663, which brought staff from Chiswick, was operated on trade plates and is here parked at Edgware station, probably on a lunchtime shopping trip. It was fitted with an STL3 body (recoded 3/3), and remained in pre-1950 livery which was a rarity by 1955. *A.B. Cross*

Apart from an experimental batch of eleven vehicles (342–352) all STLs numbered below 609 were originally fitted with petrol engines but those with preselective gearboxes were given new oil engines in 1939. Withdrawal of oil engined pre-war STLs started in 1949 and was completed on 1st September 1954, although some remained in use as staff and training buses. The 'unfrozen' buses were withdrawn from passenger service during 1952, the last on 1st November but many were then used as staff buses. None of the pre-war nor wartime buses was in service on 1st January 1955 but among those still in stock and awaiting disposal was the last survivor of the original batch of experimental oilers (STL 349) and no fewer than nineteen of those which originally had petrol engines. Ten of the 'tunnel' STLs two of the forward entrance Country Bus version and twenty-four 'unfrozens' were also in stock. Among the latter were the two carrying bodies of the original LGOC design (2674, 2679: STL1/1s). Seventeen of the twenty post-war 18STL20 type were still licensed but those at Garston and Grays were withdrawn on 1st May 1955, followed by the last seven at Hertford on 1st June. The use of pre-war and 'unfrozen' STLs as trainers and staff buses ceased in June 1955.

Many pre-war STLs were sold for further service with Independents and contractors. STL 1836 was an STL11 withdrawn in May 1955 which found its way via the dealer W. North of Leeds to T. Canham of Whittlesey, Cambridgeshire, who operated it between May 1956 and March 1960. The company's monochrome grey 'livery' suits the bleak background of Peterborough bus station only too well.
Ken Glazier

Chassis:	AEC Regent 0661
Engine:	AEC A171 (indirect injection) or A173 (direct injection) 6-cylinder 7.7 litre 95 bhp oil
Transmission:	Four speed direct selection preselective (D128 Daimler or D132 AEC) with fluid flywheel; or AEC D124 4 speed crash (2648–2701)
Chassis codes:	5, 9, 1/9, 2/9, 3/9, 4/9, 10, 2/16 or 19STL (349–2513); 17STL (2648–2681); 18STL (2682–2701)
Bodywork:	LPTB (Chiswick) or Weymann (2682–2701)
Capacity:	H30/26R (959, 986: H29/23F)
Body codes:	STL1/1, 3/1, 3/3, 3/4, 5, 5/2, 6, 11, 11/1, 12, 12/1, 13, 14, 14/1, 15, 16, 16/2, 17, 17/1, 18 or STL20 (2682–2701) or 21 (2477)
Built	(survivors) 1934–1946
Number built:	2,679
Number in stock: 1.1.55: 262	Last vehicle out of stock: 4.6.56

STL		Date out of stock	STL		Date out of stock	STL		Date out of stock
349	AUC575	17.6.55	670	BLH760	5.5.55	919	CGJ33	c 11.1.55
433	AXM691	26.1.55	672	BLH730	17.6.55	930	CGJ67	24.3.55
437	AYV611	20.1.55	682	BLH737	5.5.55	932	CGJ69	7.4.55
440	AXM699	30.1.56	688	BLH764	10.1.56	935	CGJ74	31.3.55
462	AYV617	25.1.55	698	BLH755	29.6.55	949	CGJ31	10.5.55
464	AYV620	30.3.55	712	BLH784	27.6.55	951	CGJ47	10.1.56
468	AYV628	13.6.55	734	BXD421	1.7.55	955	CGJ75	4.5.55
473	AYV624	14.3.55	742	BXD451	30.3.55	959	BLH816	28.1.55
478	AYV632	25.8.55	749	BXD409	19.8.55	975	BLH829	20.4.55
503	AYV669	9.5.55	759	BXD425	27.5.55	986	BLH859	1.7.55
505	AYV686	24.3.55	762	BXD426	31.1.55	1008	BLH864	8.6.55
511	AYV698	17.1.55	777	BXD430	24.8.55	1011	BLH870	29.6.55
515	AYV660	25.8.55	798	BXD464	19.8.55	1023	BLH895	19.4.55
523	AYV676	8.6.55	802	BXD476	16.6.55	1029	BLH896	31.1.55
536	AYV705	6.1.55	804	BXD463	30.8.55	1038	BLH900	14.6.55
537	AYV706	5.5.55	808	BXD489	24.8.55	1060	CLE37	22.8.55
548	AYV710	22.4.55	814	BXD477	3.2.55	1083	CLE45	7.9.55
564	AYV735	22.2.55	827	BXD482	15.7.55	1101	CGJ98	6.1.55
570	AYV720	29.4.55	856	BXD583	3.2.55	1145	CGJ145	5.7.55
572	AYV733	4.5.55	861	CGJ20	22.8.55	1218	BXD845	21.3.55
616	AYV779	28.1.55	868	BXD594	24.3.55	1223	CLE79	4.5.55
637	AYV782	12.1.56	873	BXD584	8.6.55	1227	BLN618	1.7.55
646	AYV791	4.5.55	900	BXD607	31.3.55	1234	BUL347	1.7.55
648	BLH733	13.1.56	905	CGJ28	21.3.55	1437	CXX180	27.1.55

c Date chassis scrapped; body dismantled earlier

STL		Date out of stock	STL		Date out of stock	STL		Date out of stock
1447	CXX193	25.6.58	1787	DGX345	14.7.55	2126	DLU125	8.8.55
1458	CXX199	21.4.55	1788	DGX346	5.4.55	2166	DYL818	6.6.55
1522	CXX214	14.3.55	1791	DGX358	10.5.55	2170	DYL822	14.6.55
1527	CXX220	15.6.55	1792	DGX356	24.3.55	2177	DYL829	13.1.56
1542	CXX236	28.1.55	1793	DLU11	15.9.55	2185	DYL837	12.8.55
1545	CXX246	6.6.55	1803	DLU21	10.5.55	2194	CXR252	15.8.55
1548	CXX253	9.3.55	1806	DLU30	12.1.56	2204	CYH783	1.7.55
1570	CXX306	5.5. 55	1811	DLU31	4.1.56	2210	CYR372	24.8.55
1581	CXX292	5.1.56	1815	DLU44	15.8.55	2301	EGO355	30.1.56
1595	CXX308	19.8.55	1819	DLU195	8.8.55	2358	EGO429	16.3.55
1597	CXX325	14.3.55	1821	DLU49	15.6.55	2392	EGO434	5.5.55
1603	ELP293	11.5.55	1824	DLU205	7.4.55	2461	ELP121	5.4.55
1604	CXX328	15.3.55	1826	DLU197	20.4.55	2475	ELP132	21.3.55
1607	CXX311	29.4.55	t 1827	DLU206	15.6.55	* 2477	ELP154	4.6.56
1608	CXX312	10.1.56	1831	DLU208	5.5. 55	2484	ELP148	14.7.55
1616	CXX326	5.7.55	1832	DLU198	16.3.55	2501	ELP163	31.1.55
1622	CXX331	28.1.55	1833	DLU199	25.8.55	2505	ELP159	27.1.55
1623	CXX334	6.6.55	1834	DLU200	8.6.55	2513	ELP174	22.3.55
1629	CXX336	1.7.55	1836	DLU202	11.5.55	2648	FXT371	13.8.58
1630	CXX340	25.4.55	1840	DLU192	24.3.55	2651	FXT374	15.8.58
1638	CXX345	28.1.55	t 1850	DLU219	13.1.56	2654	FXT377	15.8.58
1639	CXX346	13.6.55	t 1852	DLU224	27.5.55	2657	FXT380	14.8.58
1642	CXX366	25.4.55	1854	DLU221	29.6.55	2658	FXT381	12.8.55
1644	CXX349	29.4.55	t 1855	DLU232	5.4.55	2659	FXT382	13.8.58
1648	CXX372	5.5. 55	t 1865	DLU230	20.4.55	2662	FXT385	16.8.58
1652	CXX358	4.5.55	t 1866	DLU237	29.6.55	2663	FXT386	18.1.56
1659	CXX357	13.1.56	t 1868	DLU233	27.4.55	2666	FXT389	s 3.5.55
1661	CXX369	4.4.55	1873	DLU268	16.6.55	2667	FXT390	15.8.58
1668	CXX371	12.1.55	t 1874	DLU241	20.4.55	2668	FXT391	19.1.56
1670	CXX370	6.6.55	t 1875	DLU234	1.2.55	2669	FXT392	s 13.6.55
1677	DGX205	30.3.55	t 1876	DLU243	13.7.55	2670	FXT393	c 16.6.55
1678	DGX206	3.6.55	1881	DLU247	25.4.55	2671	FXT394	18.1.56
1680	DGX209	10.6.55	1883	DLU288	6.6.55	2672	FXT395	14.8.55
1681	DGX217	22.4.55	1890	DLU251	22.8.55	2673	FXT396	16.8.58
1682	DGX208	4.5.55	1894	DLU250	18.8.55	2674	FXT397	25.6.58
1688	DGX254	31.1.55	1896	DLU255	15.6.55	2675	FXT398	18.1.56
1693	CXX192	9.5.55	1898	DLU256	15.8.55	2676	FXT399	20.1.56
1695	CXX381	30.3.55	1915	DLU294	24.3.55	2677	FXT400	s 31.5.55
1698	DGX218	13.6.55	1918	DLU276	30.3.55	2678	FXT401	13.8.58
1706	DGX248	8.7.55	1922	DLU300	6.6.55	2679	FXT402	s 17.3.55
1715	DGX294	15.7.55	1927	DLU286	13.5.55	2680	FXT403	13.8.58
1716	DGX262	5.1.56	1932	DLU283	7.6.55	2681	FXT404	18.1.56
1722	DGX259	22.4.55	1936	DLU299	3.5.55	2682	HGC215	4.8.55
1725	DGX268	7.6.55	1938	DLU139	15.8.55	2683	HGC216	4.8.55
1728	DGX271	18.8.55	1940	DLU295	6.1.55	2684	HGC217	13.7.55
1730	DGX273	27.6.55	1965	DLU170	27.6.55	2685	HGC218	13.7.55
1731	DGX276	13.6.55	2013	CLF885	13.7.55	2686	HGC219	3.8.55
1741	DGX281	21.3.55	2019	DGX318	10.1.56	2687	HGC220	13.7.55
1742	DGX284	20.4.55	2021	DGX327	11.2.55	2688	HGC221	13.7.55
1743	DGX282	6.1.55	2032	DGX347	10.1.56	2689	HGC222	3.8.55
1748	DGX289	24.5.55	2038	DLU23	5.1.56	2690	HGC223	10.8.55
1749	DGX290	7.3.55	2049	DLU28	14.3.55	2691	HGC224	10.8.55
1760	DGX303	6.1.56	2056	DLU55	31.1.55	2692	HGC225	4.8.55
1762	DGX305	5.4.55	2062	DLU61	19.1.56	2693	HGC226	13.7.55
1766	DGX309	22.3.55	2071	DLU70	10.6.55	2694	HGC227	4.8.55
1771	DGX314	18.8.55	2081	DLU80	19.4.55	2695	HGC228	5.8.55
1774	DGX317	14.1.55	2086	DLU85	24.5.55	2696	HGC229	10.8.55
1775	DGX325	22.3.55	2093	DLU92	3.6.55	2697	HGC230	11.8.55
1777	DGX326	5.1.56	2100	DLU99	15.7.55	2698	HGC231	13.7.55
1779	DGX332	4.1.56	2106	DLU105	4.5.55	2699	HGC232	10.8.55
1781	DGX338	21.3.55	2108	DLU107	19.1.56	2700	HGC233	5.8.55
1782	DGX339	5.9.55	2117	DLU116	12.8.55	2701	HGC234	11.8.55
1783	DGX342	7.4.55	2120	DLU119	14.6.55			
1784	DGX340	27.5.55	2124	DLU123	29.4.55			

c Date chassis scrapped; body dismantled earlier.
s Converted to service vehicles: STL 2666 to 1019J, 2669 to 1017J, 2677 to 1016J, 2679 to 1009J
t Tunnel body (STL13)
* Last pre-war STL in stock

Although intended to continue in service until 1959, the post war 4STD3s were withdrawn prematurely in 1955 following heavy service cuts. The last garage to operate them was Loughton, whose double-deck fleet consisted exclusively of the type represented here by STD 157. Ernie Roberts

STD

In 1937, London Transport decided to accelerate the replacement of the obsolescent NS class and placed a then record order for 786 buses and coaches, of which 672 were double-deckers. As the Board was barred by statute from building more than 527 bodies a year, it was necessary to find alternative suppliers. Leyland was chosen to share the body contract and the opportunity was taken to purchase complete buses so that an alternative source for chassis could also be tested. The one hundred Titans (STD 1–100) were nominally based on the standard TD4 and TD4c model Titan chassis but they were modified to meet London Transport's requirements, notably in having STL type low geared steering and revised dumb-irons so that the towing arrangements could be interchangeable with the STL. Ninety were fitted with crash gearboxes (STD 1–90) and ten with torque convertors (STD 91–100). The bodywork was also the standard Leyland metal framed product modified in detail to resemble the latest style of roof-box STL. The torque converters were replaced by standard manual gearboxes at their first overhaul. The entire batch was allocated to Hendon garage, where the majority spent their whole lives but some were transferred to Cricklewood and Victoria during the war and others spent their last couple of years at Enfield. The last were withdrawn from passenger service on 14th June 1954. STD 101–111 were part of London Transport's intake of non-standard vehicles during World War 2. They were based on 'unfrozen' TD7 chassis, whose mechanical specification was broadly similar to the earlier Titans and were the first London buses to carry wartime austerity bodywork. They were allocated to Victoria garage, where they spent their entire operational career operating on most routes from that garage. They were withdrawn prematurely in March 1951 after drivers refused to drive them any longer. STD 112–176 were standard Leyland products, purchased by the LPTB as a stop-gap until the post-war standard models could go into production. The overall appearance of these buses was very similar to the pre-war version, particularly from the front aspect where a full set of route and destination indicators was fitted. No indicators of any kind were provided at the back, which was also more heavily curved than the earlier version. At first, they were distributed in small quantities around a number of garages: Victoria, Croydon, Potters Bar, Hanwell and Loughton but those at Potters Bar and Croydon were soon replaced, followed by those at Hanwell in 1949. Leyton also received a small allocation and Victoria's were transferred to Stockwell in November 1953. Latterly the type was concentrated wholly at Loughton, until withdrawn in 1955.

Chassis:	Leyland Titan TD4 modified (1–100); Leyland Titan TD7 (101–111); Leyland Titan PD1 (112–176)
Engine:	Leyland six cylinder 8.6 litre direct injection 94 bhp; or 7.4 litre direct injection 100 bhp (112–176)
Transmission:	Leyland four speed crash (helical third speed); or Leyland four speed constant mesh (112–176)
Bodywork:	Leyland; or Park Royal (100–111)
L.T. codes:	1STD1 (1–90); 1STD1/1 (91–100); 3STD2 (101–111); 4STD3 (112–176)
Capacity:	H30/26R (101–111 UH30/26R)
Built:	1937 (1–100); 1941 (101) 1942 (102–111) 1946 (112–176)
Number built:	176
Number in stock:	1.1.55: 125 Last vehicle out of stock: 23.3.56

STD		Date out of stock	STD		Date out of stock	STD		Date out of stock
8	DLU310	16.2.55	89	DLU399	6.1.55	136	HLW65	14.7.55
10	DLU320	26.4.55	90	DLU400	22.3.55	137	HLW66	9.8.55
13	DLU323	17.5.55	91	DLU401	11.5.55	138	HLW67	23.3.56
16	DLU326	19.9.55	92	DLU402	1.2.55	139	HLW68	7.3.56
22	DLU332	24.1.55	94	DLU404	22.2.55	140	HLW69	14.7.55
24	DLU334	9.3.55	95	DLU405	22.2.55	141	HLW70	16.12.55
26	DLU336	1.2.55	96	DLU406	6.6.55	142	HLW71	7.3.56
27	DLU337	6.6.55	97	DLU407	22.3.55	143	HLW72	23.3.56
28	DLU338	25.3.55	98	DLU408	17.5.55	144	HLW73	13.10.55
30	DLU340	3.5.55	99	DLU409	22.2.55	145	HLW74	7.3.56
34	DLU344	17.5.55	100	DLU410	4.5.55	146	HLW75	14.7.55
39	DLU349	10.3.55	101	FXT405	16.9.55	147	HLW76	12.1.56
41	DLU351	29.4.55	102	FXT428	16.9.55	148	HLW77	23.3.56
42	DLU352	19.4.55	103	FXT429	14.6.55	149	HLW78	13.10.55
43	DLU353	14.6.55	104	FXT430	5.7.55	150	HLW79	13.1.56
45	DLU355	28.2.55	105	FXT431	7.9.55	151	HLW80	9.8.55
46	DLU356	24.1.55	107	FXT433	6.5.55	152	HLW81	9.8.55
50	DLU360	1.2.55	109	FXT435	16.9.55	153	HLW82	9.8.55
53	DLU363	27.1.55	112	HGF990	23.3.56	154	HLW83	16.12.55
54	DLU364	29.4.55	113	HGF991	14.7.55	155	HLW84	16.12.55
55	DLU365	3.5.55	114	HGF992	7.3.56	156	HLW85	16.12.55
56	DLU366	22.2.55	115	HGF993	12.1.56	157	HLW86	23.3.56
58	DLU368	26.4.55	116	HGF994	12.1.56	158	HLW87	13.1.56
59	DLU369	22.2.55	117	HGF995	16.12.55	159	HLW88	7.3.56
60	DLU370	27.1.55	118	HGF996	14.7.55	160	HLW89	13.1.56
62	DLU372	26.4.55	119	HGF997	23.3.56	161	HLW90	13.10.55
66	DLU376	18.2.55	120	HGF998	7.3.56	162	HLW91	23.3.56
68	DLU378	16.2.55	121	HGF999	13.10.55	163	HLW92	9.8.55
70	DLU380	22.3.55	122	HLW51	16.12.55	164	HLW93	9.8.55
71	DLU381	16.2.55	123	HLW52	23.3.56	165	HLW94	16.12.55
74	DLU384	13.1.55	124	HLW53	13.10.55	166	HLW95	9.8.55
77	DLU387	3.2.55	125	HLW54	9.8.55	167	HLW96	14.7.55
78	DLU388	11.5.55	126	HLW55	16.12.55	168	HLW97	13.1.56
79	DLU389	3.5.55	127	HLW56	23.3.56	169	HLW98	14.7.55
80	DLU390	9.3.55	128	HLW57	12.1.56	170	HLW99	9.8.55
81	DLU391	6.5.55	129	HLW58	7.3.56	171	HLW100	9.8.55
82	DLU392	19.4.55	130	HLW59	14.7.55	172	HLW101	13.10.55
83	DLU393	17.5.55	131	HLW60	7.3.56	173	HLW102	9.8.55
84	DLU394	2.3.55	132	HLW61	13.10.55	174	HLW103	9.8.55
85	DLU395	26.4.55	133	HLW62	9.8.55	175	HLW104	9.8.55
87	DLU397	13.1.55	134	HLW63	23.3 56	176	HLW105	9.8.55
88	DLU398	15.6.55	135	HLW64	13.10.55			

Despite their reputation for quality and reliability, the pre-war STDs did not attract many buyers among bus operators. One that did was STD 96 which was operated by Culling's Coaches of Claxton, Norfolk between July 1955 and November 1961. It is seen here on their stage route in Norwich in April 1960.
Ken Glazier

Former STD 140 is seen in Troger, near Split in Yugoslavia, the country to which the 4STD3s were exported after their withdrawal in 1955. D.W.K. Jones

One of London's many 'might-have-beens', G 436 spent its last days at Enfield garage working on backwater route 121 before its premature withdrawal in 1955. A peculiarity of the standard Park Royal body was the absence of a destination blind box at the front, which enforced the retention of the restricted display seen in this photograph taken at Enfield garage.
Capital Transport Collection

G

The first 435 Guys were wartime austerity buses built between 1942 and 1946 and all had been withdrawn by the summer of 1953. In 1949, Guy Motors Ltd sought to enter the post-war London market by offering London Transport a version of their Arab chassis which could be adapted to take the standard RT body. G 436 was fitted with a 10.35 litre Meadows engine, a more powerful unit than the Gardner model normally fitted to Guys. It also had an air operated preselective gearbox, bringing its specification up to or slightly beyond that of the RT. The chassis was otherwise a standard product and carried a Park Royal body of the type then being delivered in quantity to provincial operators. A second chassis was to have been ordered which would have been built to the same profile as the RTs and RTLs, so that LT designed bodywork, fully inter-changeable between the different types, could be fitted. This order was either never placed or cancelled and the second bus was never built. G 436 was delivered to Chiswick in December 1949 and went into service at Old Kent Road garage on route 173 in January 1950. It later worked at Peckham, still on route 173 and latterly at Enfield on route 121, where it stayed until withdrawn in 1955.

Chassis:	Guy Arab III
Engine:	Meadows 6DC430 6-cylinder 10.35 litre 130 bhp oil
Transmission:	Four speed air operated preselective with fluid flywheel.
Bodywork:	Park Royal
Capacity:	H30/26R
L.T. code:	4G13
Built:	1949
Number built:	436 Number in stock: 1.1.55: 1 Out of stock: 14.7.55

G		Date out of stock
436	KGK981	14.7.55

The 2RT2 was another type which suffered premature withdrawal in 1955, the majority being taken out of service between February and June. RT 124 approaches Eltham Church on route 182, operating from New Cross garage which had received the type less than three years earlier. F.G. Reynolds

RT

The RT was a development of the AEC Regent chassis as used in the STL class but with an engine design strongly influenced by Leyland practice, following London Transport's successful operation of the one hundred 1937 Leyland Titans. At the end of the 1930s London Transport adopted a policy of having large engines, with a derated power output to improve fuel economy and engine life and the engine chosen for the RT was the AEC A185 9.6 litre unit, which developed 100 bhp at 1,800 rpm. The well tried Wilson type preselective gearbox and fluid flywheel were of the type used on the STL class but were actuated by compressed air, as were the brakes. Other features of the design were flexible engine mountings, improved and lighter steering, automatic chassis lubrication, automatic brake adjusters and a low bonnet and radiator. The prototype chassis first operated in service from Hanwell garage (HW) on route 18C between 13th July and 31st December 1938 with the number ST 1140 under a six year old fifty-six seat Dodson open staircase body originally carried by TD 111. A revolutionary new design of metal framed body, built at Chiswick Works, was then fitted and the vehicle numbered RT 1. The new body was of four bay construction and notable for its graceful curves, including the combined bulkhead and front wing assembly. Roof route number boxes were carried at both front and rear. RT 1 went into service on 9th August 1939.

Meanwhile an order had been placed for a production batch of 150, subsequently increased to 338 and the intention was to manufacture up to 527 a year from 1940 onwards. Following the outbreak of war on 3rd September 1939, government restrictions

RT 62, seen in the south-east corner of Hertford bus station, was one of seven 3/2RT2/2s whose lives were given a temporary extension as replacements for the 18STL20s on route 327. Apart from the special case of RT 97/RTC 1 they were the only 2RT2s to be painted green and remained so until replaced by standard post-war RTs on 1st September 1957. The distinctive frontal features of this type were the curved lower edge of the windscreen and the seven ventilator grilles on the dash. F.W. Ivey

were placed on the construction of chassis for civilian use and the order for the last 188 was suspended. The 2RT2s (2–151) differed from RT 1 in having composite bodywork but only minor changes were made to the design and the mechanical specification was the same. Although often referred to incorrectly as 'pre-war' RTs, the RT2s were all built during the war, starting at the end of 1939 and the first did not enter service until 2nd January 1940, at Chelverton Road. Others went to Putney Bridge and Victoria. Towards the end of the programme deliveries slowed down and the last did not go into service until 1st February 1942.

In 1945 the chassis of RT 19 was remodelled as the prototype for the post-war version. This was similar to the 2RT but had a new engine, the A204, with toroidal cavity pistons and an increased power output of 125 bhp at 1,800 rpm (derated by LT to 115 bhp). The extension behind the rear axle was omitted as the platform on the new bodies was to be self-supporting. The only variations from this standard during the entire production run were those modified for Green Line (1/3RT). The RT3 bodies were also very similar in appearance to the RT2 but without a rear route number box and without the downward curve of the windscreen. Technically the bodies were more advanced, being metal framed and designed for complete interchangeability of all parts. The RT3 was a transient design as the standard body was intended to have no roof route number box at the front and an illuminated route number box under the canopy. The last hundred Park Royal (RT 752–851) and fifty Weymann (962–1011) RT3s had an interim modification incorporating a route number plate under the canopy and trafficator housings and were also made suitable for mounting on both AEC and Leyland chassis. These were recoded RT10 in about 1951. The final modified design was coded RT3/1 and appeared from October 1948, after 450 Park Royal and 300 Weymann bodied buses had been built. The trafficator housing on these and the RT10s was plated over and the equipment was not fitted to most vehicles, although 135 RT3/1s (and sixty-five RTLs) were fitted with them experimentally for a time from November 1949. These vehicles were also fitted with drivers' cab heaters, a feature which was eventually extended to the whole class. From February 1949 modifications were made to the body mountings to make them compatible with the SRT class for which a new code RT8 was allocated. Later Green Line versions were coded RT8/1 and bodies built after December 1952 had a modified bulkhead and were classified RT8/2.

Delivery of chassis from AEC began at the end of March 1946 but there were serious delays in the manufacture of bodies by Park Royal and Weymann and the first 3RT3 (RT 402) did not go into service until 10th May 1947, at Leyton garage. Because of these delays, London Transport ordered additional bodies, 250 from the Saunders Engineering and Shipyard Company of Beaumaris, Anglesey and 120 from Cravens Ltd of Sheffield. The Saunders bodies (classified RT3/3) were virtually identical to the RT3, the distinguishing feature being their offside route number plate which was further back; but the Cravens (RT3/4) were standard products with five bay construction, a more upright front and more curved back but with a standard indicator layout with roof route number box. The Saunders were delivered between September 1948 and February 1951 and the Cravens between September 1948 and April 1950. Other odd men out were RTs 2116–2121 which received second hand bodies recovered from the works float when new in 1950. A late arrival, also in 1950, was RT 657 whose original body and registration number were appropriated for prototype RTL 501 in 1948. Twenty-two float bodies were built altogether, fifteen being the last RT bodies built by Park Royal, which were stored on redundant SRT chassis at New Cross garage until required for the new overhaul system at Aldenham in 1955.

A number of experiments have been carried out on RTs. Five were fitted experimentally with Miller type RV7 direct selection electro-hydraulic gearboxes (RTs 778 in September 1948, 902 in December 1948 and 2207, 2208 and 2273 in May, June and July 1949). In May 1953 RT 3684 was fitted with a revised RV16 gearbox. These experiments eventually led to the transmission adopted on the Routemaster. The equipment was removed from RT 902 when overhauled in 1957 but the others retained theirs, although under new fleet numbers 4426, 4343, 4455, 1172 and 2134 respectively. Other experiments included straight-through silencers (RTs 3647, 3653, 3660, 3664, 3670 and 3671 early in 1953), dry automatic clutches (RTs 2707 and 3586 in the summer of 1953 and later a modified design on RTs 3906 and 3923) and turbocharged engine (RT 3326 in January 1956). RT 3937 was fitted with flashing trafficators similar to the new design on RM 1 in mid-1956 and following further experiments on eighty-seven RTs (and thirty-eight RFs) a programme of converting all buses was started in 1959. Before going into service, RT 769 spent nearly a year at the Motor Industry Research Association's vehicle proving establishment at Lindley near Nuneaton from October 1948, where further tests on other vehicles took place later. RT 3995 was withdrawn from service in March 1951, soon after being licensed, and became a permanent test bed for the Chiswick Works experimental shop.

A number of RTs have also been used for overseas trade promotion visits, the first being RTs 1692, 1702, 3070 and 3114 which made a grand tour of continental Europe in 1950, covering about 4,000 miles, on loan to the Festival of Britain authorities. In 1952 RTs 2775 and 2776, in company with RTL 1307, were hired by the British Travel and Holidays Association to make a 12,000 mile tour of north America. RT 2776 was used to give rides, for which duty it was equipped with additional ventilators to combat the heat of the southern States. Two were fitted in the front dome, in the form of semi-circular grilles and a third under the canopy. Other trips have been made by RT 3710 (with RTL 1459) to Zurich and Malmo in 1953; RT 4760 to Maastricht in 1954; RT 2422 (with RTL 1486) to Holland in 1957 and Helsinki again in 1957. All these vehicles retained their GB plates and their individual identity when overhauled.

Above **RT 94**, a 1/2RT2/1, was one of many of the type which saw out their last few years as trainers, in which role it is seen at Amersham garage. It was one of the those which had been fitted with pillar-mounted route number plates in 1946. Peter J. Relf

Left The pure RT3 body could be distinguished from other roof-box types by the valance around the canopy and the pillar-mounted route number plate. These plates were often not used in later years, which was the case when Norwood's RT 505 was photographed at Crystal Palace Parade, with the grand structure of the as yet still intact High Level station in the background. Peter J. Relf

Post-war RT deliveries continued until November 1954, when the number of RTs in stock reached its maximum of 4,820, the last into stock being Weymann RT 4794. Eighty-one of the new green RTs did not enter service immediately but went straight into store at Loughton garage, as there was no immediate use for them. They were RTs 4543–4556, 4727–4759 and 4761–4794. Fourteen of the unused buses in store at Loughton were licensed for service in May 1955 to replace the 18STL20s and a few others were brought out from time to time but the bulk remained in store until March 1958, when they began to be licensed to replace older post-war vehicles which were then sold. The last RT to be licensed was RT 4773 at Northfleet in August 1959.

Withdrawal of RTs had started as early as 1946 when the chassis of RT 1 was scrapped, its body being used on post-war prototype RT 19 indirectly replacing that of RT 66 which was destroyed during the war. RT 22 overturned in icy conditions on Wimbledon Hill in 1951 and was a write off. RT 97 was converted to RTC 1 in 1949 and RT 85 was destroyed by fire while in service on route 74 in May 1949. RT 19, still with the body of RT 1, was transferred to the Miscellaneous vehicle fleet in September 1954 as an instruction chassis and renumbered 1020J. The chassis was later scrapped and the body mounted on SRT 45 until this too was scrapped and replaced by the chassis of RT 1420 in 1956 as 1037J. Withdrawal of most of the remaining RT2s was started in February 1955 and all but seven had gone by the end of May. Eight (RTs 36, 62, 79, 93, 114, 128 and 137 – joined later by RT 133) were retained for use on route 327 at Hertford garage which crossed a bridge on which there was a weight restriction disqualifying the use of the heavier post-war type. All were repainted green, except RT 133 which was therefore the last red RT2 in service. These were withdrawn on 1st September 1957. Many 2RT2s were retained as trainers or staff buses but were later gradually replaced by surplus RTLs and only a handful were left at the end of 1962. Some 2RT2s saw further service with provincial operators, mainly small Independents. RT 106 was transferred to the Miscellaneous fleet as a turnover vehicle, numbered 1036TV.

Withdrawal of post-war RTs began in May 1955 following a series of service cuts, when fifty of the non-standard Cravens were withdrawn by Central Buses; the last red ones were taken out of service in April 1956. The first green example was withdrawn when the body of RT 1420 was destroyed in a low bridge accident at Norbiton station when on Green Line relief duty. Its chassis was later fitted with the body of RT 1 and became 1037J. Although twenty-three red Cravens were repainted green to cover overhauls between March and May 1956, all the green examples were withdrawn by 17th October 1956 when the last four finished at Windsor. Continuing cuts led to a start being made on the withdrawal of standard RTs at the beginning of 1958 and this was given a boost by the severe service cuts which followed the seven week bus strike later that year. The first withdrawals under this programme were the oldest chassis but this led to the withdrawal of some bodies as young as four years old and the criterion was changed to withdrawal of the oldest bodies. The withdrawal programme was slowed in 1959 as RTs and RTLs were used in the first three stages of the trolleybus conversion because Routemaster deliveries were running late.

In 1956 eighty-seven RTs (and thirty-eight RFs) were fitted experimentally with trafficators of the type pioneered on the RM class. The experiment was successful and was extended to the whole fleet 1959 and 1960. Those RTs, mainly RT3s, which did not have the arrows incorporated into the rear light fitting above the registration plate, were fitted with separate flashing units on the near- and offside of the rear panel. The combined arrows on the remainder were not satisfactory, however, and these were given separate left turn arrows from 1962.

The fifty-seven Green Line RTs were fitted with saloon heaters in 1959, being recoded 1/3RT at this time, and a further twenty-eight were similarly fitted and repainted in Green Line livery in 1960 for use as scheduled duplicates. The fitting of heaters was extended to all Country Buses between September 1961 and June 1963.

Newly overhauled surplus 3RT3s figured prominently in the first stage of the Trolleybus Conversion Scheme in March 1959 and RT 265, seen in the throes of a crew changeover outside the garage, was typical of Carshalton's starting allocation of motor buses.
Lens of Sutton

The two features which set the RT10 apart from the RT3 when viewed from the offside were the sealed trafficator housing immediately behind the driver's cab door, and the slight upsweep at the bottom of the dash panel, designed to clear the dumbiron of an RTL. RT 801 was one of the hundred of this type built by Park Royal eleven years before this photograph was taken at the old Twickenham station in June 1959. G. Mead

The appearance of RT 4108, at Windsor Castle, was typical of the standard RT3/1 and RT8 bodywork supplied by both Park Royal and Weymann between 1948 and 1954. The layout of the colours for the Weymann bodied Country Bus examples was the same as for their Central Bus counterparts, except that green rather than black was used for the mudguards.
F.G. Reynolds

When RT 353 ran for the first time at Cricklewood in March 1948, it carried an RT3 body but by the time of this photograph in Katharine Street, Croydon, the overhaul float system had substituted a standard RT8. Peter J. Relf

Although classified RT8/1, the RTs supplied for the Romford and Grays Green Line services were identical to standard buses except for their special livery. The cream relief colour was replaced by the light green of the standard coach livery, and a raised metal 'GREEN LINE' bullseye was carried on each of the side upper deck panels. The Minories Trolleybus and Coach station at Aldgate in September 1962 provides the almost inevitable background to RT 3244, one of the first batch, bodied by Weymann in 1950. Photofive Transport Enterprises

The rear view of the post-war RT body changed little over the years, only the application of circular rear reflectors in 1954 and the later modifications when trafficators were fitted having any effect. The basic nature of these 'coaches' is evident in the absence of platform doors on RT 3253 at Aldgate. A.B. Cross

Above **The RTs carrying former SRT bodies were indistinguishable from the pure product, as can be seen in this study of RT 4515 at Hawley, which inherited the body from SRT 134.** Malcolm Papes Collection

Facing page upper **The offside route number plate on the RT3/3 Saunders bodies was set midway between the rearmost saloon window and the rear of the body, providing a useful recognition feature on an otherwise standard looking body. RT 3100, originally a 3RT8, was photographed at the Embankment terminus on 19th August 1958, the last day of operation of route 50A, a former tram route.** A.B. Cross

Facing page lower **From this angle, in Station Road West Croydon, the Saunders body of RT 457 could be mistaken for an RT10, but a sharp-eyed observer would note that the bottom of the front dash panel does not have the upsweep needed to clear the dumbiron of a Leyland chassis. In the background is Country Bus RT 3126, a 3RT8, on route 409.** A.B. Cross

The 120 RT3/4 bodies supplied by Cravens Ltd between 1948 and 1950 were the most distinctive of the RT family, being virtually standard products of the Sheffield factory with five bay construction and a more upright front profile. Only the standard design of driver's cab of RT 1453 and its low bonnet line mark it out as a member of the class.
J.H. Aston

The Craven RTs had a brief spell of extended use during the railway strike in the summer of 1955 before being withdrawn irrevocably. RT 1467 was allocated to Dunton Green, where it was photographed on 22nd August 1955.
W.R. Legg

RT 31, parked in front of a Country Bus RT on route 301 in Kingsbury Square, Aylesbury, was one of a number of RTs purchased by the Buckinghamshire independent operator Red Rover.
Ken Glazier

The independent Osborne's of Tollesbury, Essex, built up a small fleet of former London Transport buses in the 1960s which retained a strong London flavour thanks to the company's handsome red and cream colour scheme. Former RT 405 was photographed in Church Street, Tollesbury.
Ken Glazier

Facing page upper **The Potteries was another centre for discarded London Transport vehicles, which were popular with the many independent operators in the area. Craven bodied former RT 1432 is seen in Hanley working for Thomas Beckett, in October 1962.** Ken Glazier

Facing page lower **The spruce, fully lined out, paintwork of A1's HLW 162 considerably brightens the drab surroundings of Kilmarnock bus station during its layover on the Kilmarnock route. RT 175 was a 3RT3 bodied by Park Royal in 1947 and would originally have had a roof route number box but, as was often the case, the box has been removed as redundant by its new owner. It was less common for major alterations to be made by smaller operators to the main destination and 'via' boxes but in this case a typical Scottish design of box has been substituted.** Ken Glazier

Above **No fewer than thirty Cravens were bought by Dundee Corporation in 1956, to accelerate its tram replacement programme. The Scottish municipality continued the use of roof route number boxes but removed the large intermediate point box and installed rubber mounted glazing for the small destination display. These modifications, the absence of wheel trims and the rather uninspired dark green and white livery combine to give former RT 1410, now numbered 218, a less than perfect appearance while laying over alongside redundant tram track in High Street, Dundee, on the former tram route to Maryfield.** Ken Glazier

Chassis: AEC Regent III 0661 (2–151); AEC Regent 3RT 0961 (remainder)
Engine: AEC A185 (2–151) 100 bhp or A204 9.6 litre direct injection oil 125bhp
(derated to 115bhp)
Transmission: AEC D140 4-speed air operated preselective with fluid flywheel
Bodywork: LPTB (2–151); Park Royal (originally 152–401, 652–961, 1522–2115, 2117–
2121, 2522–3041, 4268–4556, 4569–4684, 4795–4825); Weymann (originally
402–651, 962–1151, 2116, 2122–2521, 3042–4217, 4557–4568, 4685–4794);
Saunders (1152–1401, 4218–4267); Cravens (1402–1521)
Capacity: H56R
L.T. chassis code: 3RT (1/3RT if modified for Green Line)
L.T. Body codes: RT3: 152–656, 658–851, 962–1011, 2116–2121: first post-war roof-box design
(752–851 and 962–1011 with canopy route plate and trafficator housings.)
RT3/1: 852–945, 1012–1111: first design without roof box.
RT3/3: 1152–1401, 4218–4267: Roofbox bodies by Saunders.
RT3/4: 1402–1521 non-standard roofbox bodies by Cravens.
RT8: 657, 946–961, 1112–1151, 1522–2829, 3042–3223, 3260–3527, 3842–4217, 4397–
4488, 4510–4556: as RT3/1 but with modified mountings.
RT8/1: As RT8 but modified for Green Line, including saloon heaters.
RT8/2: 2830–3041, 3528–3841, 4268–4396, 4557–4825: improved version of RT8.
RT10: Code applied to last 150 RT3 bodies (RT 752 etc.) when mountings modified
to allow use on RTL chassis from October 1956.
Built: 1939–1942 (2–151); 1947–1954 (rest)
Number built: 4825
Number in stock: 1.1.55: 4820   31.12.62: 4456

RT		Date out of stock	RT		Date out of stock	RT		Date out of stock
2	FXT177	22.12.55	44	FXT219		84	FXT259	20.12.55
3	FXT178	20.12.55	45	FXT220		86	FXT261	
4	FXT179	27.9.60	46	FXT221	26.9.60	87	FXT262	22.12.55
5	FXT180		47	FXT222		88	FXT263	
6	FXT181	23.9.60	48	FXT223	26.9.60	89	FXT264	3.8.62
7	FXT182	23.9.60	49	FXT224	21.9.60	90	FXT265	
8	FXT183	23.9.60	50	FXT225	26.9.60	91	FXT266	29.9.60
9	FXT184	26.9.60	51	FXT226	20.9.60	92	FXT267	
10	FXT185		52	FXT227		93	FXT268	27.9.60
11	FXT186		53	FXT228		94	FXT269	
12	FXT187	23.9.60	54	FXT229	20.12.55	95	FXT270	
13	FXT188	22.11.62	55	FXT230		96	FXT271	
14	FXT189	20.9.60	56	FXT231	2.2.60	98	FXT273	
15	FXT190		57	FXT232	13.4.60	99	FXT274	20.9.60
16	FXT191	23.9.60	58	FXT233	1.4.60	100	FXT275	26.9.60
17	FXT192	25.3.60	59	FXT234	24.6.55	101	FXT276	27.9.60
18	FXT193	26.9.60	60	FXT235		102	FXT277	
20	FXT195	20.9.60	61	FXT236	22.12.55	103	FXT278	13.4.60
21	FXT196		62	FXT237	29.11.62	104	FXT279	
23	FXT198	26.9.60	63	FXT238		105	FXT280	25.3.60
24	FXT199	27.9.60	64	FXT239	2.12.60	106	FXT281	s 19.12.55
25	FXT200	21.12.55	65	FXT240	21.11.61	107	FXT282	
26	FXT201	13.4.60	66	FXT241	27.9.60	108	FXT283	21.12.55
27	FXT202	20.12.55	67	FXT242	21.9.60	109	FXT284	
28	FXT203	13.4.60	68	FXT243	27.9.60	110	FXT285	
29	FXT204	27.9.60	69	FXT244	26.9.60	111	FXT286	
30	FXT205		70	FXT245		112	FXT287	20.9.60
31	FXT206	21.12.55	71	FXT246	20.9.60	113	FXT288	
32	FXT207	20.12.55	72	FXT247		114	FXT289	
33	FXT208		73	FXT248	10.8.59	115	FXT290	
34	FXT209	29.11.62	74	FXT249	2.2.60	116	FXT291	
35	FXT210	20.9.60	75	FXT250	29.11.62	117	FXT292	26.9.60
36	FXT211		76	FXT251	21.12.55	118	FXT293	
37	FXT212	21.9.60	77	FXT252	28.12.62	119	FXT294	
38	FXT213	20.9.60	78	FXT253		120	FXT295	
39	FXT214		79	FXT254		121	FXT296	
40	FXT215	21.12.55	80	FXT255		122	FXT297	20.9.60
41	FXT216		81	FXT256		123	FXT298	
42	FXT217		82	FXT257		124	FXT299	25.3.60
43	FXT218	20.9.60	83	FXT258		125	FXT300	22.12.55

RT		Date out of stock	RT		Date out of stock	RT		Date out of stock
126	FXT301	25.3.60	197	HLW184		268	HLX85	
127	FXT302		198	HLW185		269	HLX86	
128	FXT303		199	HLW186	17.10.58	270	HLX87	
129	FXT304	20.2.61	200	HLW187		271	HLX88	
130	FXT305		201	HLW188		272	HLX89	20.11.58
131	FXT306	17.10.60	202	HLW189		273	HLX90	
132	FXT307		203	HLW190		274	HLX91	
133	FXT308		204	HLW191	12.12.58	275	HLX92	
134	FXT309	3.10.60	205	HLW192	1.4.59	276	HLX93	
135	FXT310	20.9.60	206	HLW193		277	HLX94	
136	FXT311	23.6.60	207	HLW194		278	HLX95	
137	FXT312		208	HLW195	27.2.58	279	HLX96	
138	FXT313	23.9.60	209	HLW196		280	HLX97	
139	FXT314	20.12.55	210	HLW197		281	HLX98	
140	FXT315	22.12.55	211	HLW198		282	HLX99	
141	FXT316		212	HLW199	20.11.58	283	HLX100	
142	FXT317		213	HLW200	12.12.58	284	HLX101	
143	FXT318	1.4.60	214	HLW201		285	HLX102	
144	FXT319		215	HLW202		286	HLX103	
145	FXT320	23.9.60	216	HLW203		287	HLX104	
146	FXT321	21.9.60	217	HLW204	20.11.58	288	HLX105	
147	FXT322		218	HLW205		289	HLX106	
148	FXT323	28.9.60	219	HLW206		290	HLX107	
149	FXT324	20.12.55	220	HLW207		291	HLX108	
150	FXT325		221	HLW208	24.12.58	292	HLX109	
151	FXT326	26.11.62	222	HLW209		293	HLX110	
152	HLW139	28.2.58	223	HLW210		294	HLX111	
153	HLW140		224	HLW211		295	HLX112	
154	HLW141	21.3.58	225	HLW212		296	HLX113	
155	HLW142	20.2.58	226	HLW213		297	HLX114	
156	HLW143	25.3.58	227	HLW214	1.4.59	298	HLX115	
157	HLW144	12.6.58	228	HLW215		299	HLX116	
158	HLW145	21.4.58	229	HLW216		300	HLX117	
159	HLW146	8.7.58	230	HLW217		301	HLX118	
160	HLW147		231	HLW218	17.7.59	302	HLX119	
161	HLW148	21.4.58	232	HLW219	3.4.59	303	HLX120	
162	HLW149	2.5.58	233	HLW220		304	HLX121	
163	HLW150	21.3.58	234	HLW221	27.2.58	305	HLX122	
164	HLW151	12.6.58	235	HLW222		306	HLX123	
165	HLW152	2.5.58	236	HLW223		307	HLX124	
166	HLW153	25.1.58	237	HLW224		308	HLX125	1.2.58
167	HLW154		238	HLW225		309	HLX126	
168	HLW155	25.4.58	239	HLW226		310	HLX127	
169	HLW156	25.1.58	240	HLW227		311	HLX128	
170	HLW157	23.6.58	241	HLW228		312	HLX129	
171	HLW158	2.5.58	242	HLW229	24.12.58	313	HLX130	
172	HLW159	25.3.58	243	HLW230	22.4.58	314	HLX131	
173	HLW160	25.4.58	244	HLW231		315	HLX132	
174	HLW161	25.3.58	245	HLW232	1.2.58	316	HLX133	
175	HLW162	24.7.58	246	HLW233		317	HLX134	
176	HLW163	25.1.58	247	HLW234		318	HLX135	
177	HLW164	25.4.58	248	HLW235		319	HLX136	
178	HLW165	15.7.58	249	HLW236		320	HLX137	
179	HLW166	23.6.58	250	HLW237		321	HLX138	6.2.59
180	HLW167	12.2.58	251	HLW238	27.2.58	322	HLX139	20.11.58
181	HLW168		252	HLW239		323	HLX140	
182	HLW169		253	HLW240		324	HLX141	
183	HLW170	20.11.58	254	HLW241		325	HLX142	28.1.59
184	HLW171		255	HLW242		326	HLX143	
185	HLW172		256	HLW243		327	HLX144	
186	HLW173		257	HLW244	20.11.58	328	HLX145	19.7.62
187	HLW174		258	HLW245	17.10.58	329	HLX146	
188	HLW175		259	HLW246		330	HLX147	
189	HLW176		260	HLW247		331	HLX148	
190	HLW177		261	HLW248		332	HLX149	
191	HLW178		262	HLW249		333	HLX150	
192	HLW179		263	HLW250		334	HLX151	
193	HLW180		264	HLX81		335	HLX152	20.11.58
194	HLW181		265	HLX82		336	HLX153	
195	HLW182		266	HLX83		337	HLX154	
196	HLW183		267	HLX84		338	HLX155	

RT		Date out of stock	RT		Date out of stock	RT		Date out of stock
339	HLX156		410	HLX227	12.6.58	481	HLX298	
340	HLX157		411	HLX228	23.6.58	482	HLX299	
341	HLX158		412	HLX229	21.4.58	483	HLX300	
342	HLX159		413	HLX230	21.5.58	484	HLX301	
343	HLX160		414	HLX231	23.6.58	485	HLX302	27.2.58
344	HLX161		415	HLX232	21.3.58	486	HLX303	
345	HLX162		416	HLX233	21.4.58	487	HLX304	
346	HLX163		417	HLX234	25.4.58	488	HLX305	
347	HLX164		418	HLX235	23.6.58	489	HLX306	
348	HLX165		419	HLX236	12.6.58	490	HLX307	
349	HLX166		420	HLX237	12.6.58	491	HLX308	
350	HLX167		421	HLX238	25.3.58	492	HLX309	
351	HLX168	17.10.58	422	HLX239		493	HLX310	
352	HLX169		423	HLX240	25.1.58	494	HLX311	
353	HLX170		424	HLX241	21.4.58	495	HLX312	
354	HLX171		425	HLX242		496	HLX313	
355	HLX172		426	HLX243	28.2.58	497	HLX314	
356	HLX173		427	HLX244	23.6.58	498	HLX315	
357	HLX174		428	HLX245	15.7.58	499	HLX316	
358	HLX175		429	HLX246		500	HLX317	
359	HLX176	20.11.58	430	HLX247		501	HLX318	
360	HLX177		431	HLX248		502	HLX319	
361	HLX178		432	HLX249	4.2.59	503	HLX320	
362	HLX179		433	HLX250		504	HLX321	
363	HLX180		434	HLX251		505	HLX322	
364	HLX181		435	HLX252		506	HLX323	
365	HLX182		436	HLX253		507	HLX324	
366	HLX183		437	HLX254		508	HLX325	
367	HLX184		438	HLX255		509	HLX326	
368	HLX185		439	HLX256		510	HLX327	
369	HLX186		440	HLX257		511	HLX328	
370	HLX187		441	HLX258		512	HLX329	
371	HLX188		442	HLX259		513	HLX330	
372	HLX189		443	HLX260		514	HLX331	
373	HLX190		444	HLX261		515	HLX332	
374	HLX191		445	HLX262		516	HLX333	
375	HLX192		446	HLX263		517	HLX334	
376	HLX193		447	HLX264		518	HLX335	
377	HLX194		448	HLX265		519	HLX336	
378	HLX195		449	HLX266		520	HLX337	
379	HLX196		450	HLX267		521	HLX338	4.2.59
380	HLX197		451	HLX268		522	HLX339	
381	HLX198		452	HLX269		523	HLX340	
382	HLX199		453	HLX270		524	HLX341	
383	HLX200		454	HLX271	17.10.58	525	HLX342	
384	HLX201		455	HLX272		526	HLX343	
385	HLX202	17.10.58	456	HLX273		527	HLX344	
386	HLX203		457	HLX274		528	HLX345	
387	HLX204		458	HLX275		529	HLX346	
388	HLX205		459	HLX276		530	HLX347	6.2.59
389	HLX206		460	HLX277		531	HLX348	
390	HLX207		461	HLX278		532	HLX349	
391	HLX208		462	HLX279		533	HLX350	
392	HLX209		463	HLX280		534	HLX351	
393	HLX210		464	HLX281		535	HLX352	
394	HLX211		465	HLX282		536	HLX353	
395	HLX212		466	HLX283		537	HLX354	
396	HLX213		467	HLX284		538	HLX355	
397	HLX214		468	HLX285		539	HLX356	
398	HLX215		469	HLX286		540	HLX357	
399	HLX216		470	HLX287		541	HLX358	
400	HLX217		471	HLX288		542	HLX359	
401	HLX218		472	HLX289		543	HLX360	
402	HLX219	25.1.58	473	HLX290		544	HLX361	
403	HLX220	12.6.58	474	HLX291		545	HLX362	
404	HLX221	28.1.58	475	HLX292		546	HLX363	
405	HLX222	25.1.58	476	HLX293		547	HLX364	
406	HLX223	2.5.58	477	HLX294		548	HLX365	
407	HLX224	28.1.58	478	HLX295		549	HLX366	
408	HLX225	12.6.58	479	HLX296		550	HLX367	
409	HLX226	18.7.58	480	HLX297		551	HLX368	

RT

552	HLX369
553	HLX370
554	HLX371
555	HLX372
556	HLX373
557	HLX374
558	HLX375
559	HLX376
560	HLX377
561	HLX378
562	HLX379
563	HLX380
564	HLX381
565	HLX382
566	HLX383
567	HLX384
568	HLX385
569	HLX386
570	HLX387
571	HLX388
572	HLX389
573	HLX390
574	HLX391
575	HLX392
576	HLX393
577	HLX394
578	HLX395
579	HLX396
580	HLX397
581	HLX398
582	HLX399
583	HLX400
584	HLX401
585	HLX402
586	HLX403
587	HLX404
588	HLX405
589	HLX406
590	HLX407
591	HLX408
592	HLX409
593	HLX410
594	HLX411
595	HLX412
596	HLX413
597	HLX414
598	HLX415
599	HLX416
600	HLX417
601	HLX418
602	HLX419
603	HLX420
604	HLX421
605	HLX422
606	HLX423
607	HLX424
608	HLX425
609	HLX426
610	HLX427
611	HLX428
612	HLX429
613	HLX430
614	HLX431
615	HLX432
616	HLX433
617	HLX434
618	HLX435
619	HLX436
620	HLX437
621	HLX438
622	JXC430

RT

623	JXC431
624	JXC432
625	JXC433
626	JXC434
627	JXC435
628	JXC436
629	JXC437
630	JXC438
631	JXC439
632	JXC440
633	JXC441
634	JXC442
635	JXC443
636	JXC444
637	JXC445
638	JXC446
639	JXC447
640	JXC448
641	JXC449
642	JXC450
643	JXC451
644	JXC452
645	JXC453
646	JXC454
647	JXC455
648	JXC456
649	JXC457
650	JXC458
651	JXC459
652	JXC15
653	JXC16
654	JXC17
655	JXC18
656	JXC19
657	KLB712
658	JXC21
659	JXC22
660	JXC23
661	JXC24
662	JXC25
663	JXC26
664	JXC27
665	JXC28
666	JXC29
667	JXC30
668	JXC31
669	JXC32
670	JXC33
671	JXC34
672	JXC35
673	JXC36
674	JXC37
675	JXC38
676	JXC39
677	JXC40
678	JXC41
679	JXC42
680	JXC43
681	JXC44
682	JXC45
683	JXC46
684	JXC47
685	JXC48
686	JXC49
687	JXC50
688	JXC51
689	JXC52
690	JXC53
691	JXC54
692	JXC55
693	JXC56

RT

694	JXC57
695	JXC58
696	JXC59
697	JXC60
698	JXC61
699	JXC62
700	JXC63
701	JXC64
702	JXC65
703	JXC66
704	JXC67
705	JXC68
706	JXC69
707	JXC70
708	JXC71
709	JXC72
710	JXC73
711	JXC74
712	JXC75
713	JXC76
714	JXC77
715	JXC78
716	JXC79
717	JXC80
718	JXC81
719	JXC82
720	JXC83
721	JXC84
722	JXC85
723	JXC86
724	JXC87
725	JXC88
726	JXC89
727	JXC90
728	JXC91
729	JXC92
730	JXC93
731	JXC94
732	JXC95
733	JXC96
734	JXC97
735	JXC98
736	JXC99
737	JXC100
738	JXC101
739	JXC102
740	JXC103
741	JXC104
742	JXC105
743	JXC106
744	JXC107
745	JXC108
746	JXC109
747	JXC110
748	JXC111
749	JXC112
750	JXC113
751	JXC114
752	JXC115
753	JXC116
754	JXC117
755	JXC118
756	JXC119
757	JXC120
758	JXC121
759	JXC122
760	JXC123
761	JXC124
762	JXC125
763	JXC126
764	JXC127

RT		RT		Date out of stock	RT	
765	JXC128	836	JXN214		907	JXN285
766	JXC129	837	JXN215		908	JXN286
767	JXC130	838	JXN216		909	JXN287
768	JXC131	839	JXN217		910	JXN288
769	JXC132	840	JXN218		911	JXN289
770	JXC133	841	JXN219		912	JXN290
771	JXC134	842	JXN220		913	JXN291
772	JXC135	843	JXN221		914	JXN292
773	JXC136	844	JXN222		915	JXN293
774	JXC137	845	JXN223		916	JXN294
775	JXC138	846	JXN224		917	JXN295
776	JXC139	847	JXN225		918	JXN296
777	JXC140	848	JXN226		919	JXN297
778	JXC141	849	JXN227		920	JXN298
779	JXC142	850	JXN228		921	JXN299
780	JXC143	851	JXN229		922	JXN300
781	JXC144	852	JXN230		923	JXN301
782	JXC145	853	JXN231		924	JXN302
783	JXC146	854	JXN232		925	JXN303
784	JXC147	855	JXN233		926	JXN304
785	JXC148	856	JXN234		927	JXN305
786	JXC149	857	JXN235		928	JXN306
787	JXC150	858	JXN236		929	JXN307
788	JXC151	859	JXN237		930	JXN308
789	JXC152	860	JXN238		931	JXN309
790	JXC153	861	JXN239		992	JXN310
791	JXC154	862	JXN240		933	JXN311
792	JXC155	863	JXN241		934	JXN312
793	JXC156	864	JXN242		935	JXN325
794	JXC157	865	JXN243		936	JXN326
795	JXC158	866	JXN244		937	JXN327
796	JXC159	867	JXN245		938	JXN328
797	JXC160	868	JXN246		939	JXN329
798	JXC161	869	JXN247	10.5.61	940	JXN330
799	JXC162	870	JXN248		941	JXN331
800	JXC163	871	JXN249		942	JXN332
801	JXC164	872	JXN250		943	JXN343
802	JXN180	873	JXN251		944	JXN345
803	JXN181	874	JXN252		945	JXN346
804	JXN182	875	JXN253		946	KGK917
805	JXN183	876	JXN254		947	KGK918
806	JXN184	877	JXN255		948	KGK919
807	JXN185	878	JXN256		949	KGK920
808	JXN186	879	JXN257		950	KGK921
809	JXN187	880	JXN258		951	KGK922
810	JXN188	881	JXN259		952	KGK923
811	JXN189	882	JXN260		953	KGK924
812	JXN190	883	JXN261		954	KGK925
813	JXN191	884	JXN262		955	KGK926
814	JXN192	885	JXN263		956	KGK927
815	JXN193	886	JXN264		957	KGK928
816	JXN194	887	JXN265		958	KGU232
817	JXN195	888	JXN266		959	KGU233
818	JXN196	889	JXN267		960	KGU234
819	JXN197	890	JXN268		961	KGU235
820	JXN198	891	JXN269		962	JXC490
821	JXN199	892	JXN270		963	JXC491
822	JXN200	893	JXN271		964	JXC492
823	JXN201	894	JXN272		965	JXC493
824	JXN202	895	JXN273		966	JXC494
825	JXN203	896	JXN274		967	JXC495
826	JXN204	897	JXN275		968	JXC496
827	JXN205	898	JXN276		969	JXC497
828	JXN206	899	JXN277		970	JXC498
829	JXN207	900	JXN278		971	JXC499
830	JXN208	901	JXN279		972	JXC500
831	JXN209	902	JXN280		973	JXN1
832	JXN210	903	JXN281		974	JXN2
833	JXN211	904	JXN282		975	JXN3
834	JXN212	905	JXN283		976	JXN4
835	JXN213	906	JXN284		977	JXN5

RT		RT		Date out of stock	RT		Date out of stock
978	JXN6	1049	JXN77		1120	JXN148	
979	JXN7	1050	JXN78		1121	JXN149	
980	JXN8	1051	JXN79		1122	JXN150	
981	JXN9	1052	JXN80		1123	JXN151	
982	JXN10	1053	JXN81		1124	JXN152	
983	JXN11	1054	JXN82		1125	JXN153	
984	JXN12	1055	JXN83		1126	JXN154	
985	JXN13	1056	JXN84		1127	JXN155	
986	JXN14	1057	JXN85		1128	JXN156	
987	JXN15	1058	JXN86		1129	JXN157	
988	JXN16	1059	JXN87		1130	JXN158	
989	JXN17	1060	JXN88		1131	JXN159	
990	JXN18	1061	JXN89		1132	JXN160	
991	JXN19	1062	JXN90		1133	JXN161	
992	JXN20	1063	JXN91		1134	JXN162	
993	JXN21	1064	JXN92		1135	JXN163	
994	JXN22	1065	JXN93		1136	JXN164	
995	JXN23	1066	JXN94		1137	JXN165	
996	JXN24	1067	JXN95	11.9.62	1138	JXN166	
997	JXN25	1068	JXN96		1139	JXN167	
998	JXN26	1069	JXN97		1140	JXN168	
999	JXN27	1070	JXN98		1141	JXN169	
1000	JXN28	1071	JXN99		1142	JXN170	
1001	JXN29	1072	JXN100		1143	JXN171	
1002	JXN30	1073	JXN101		1144	JXN172	
1003	JXN31	1074	JXN102		1145	JXN173	
1004	JXN32	1075	JXN103		1146	JXN174	
1005	JXN33	1076	JXN104		1147	JXN175	
1006	JXN34	1077	JXN105		1148	JXN176	
1007	JXN35	1078	JXN106		1149	JXN177	
1008	JXN36	1079	JXN107		1150	JXN178	
1009	JXN37	1080	JXN108		1151	JXN179	
1010	JXN38	1081	JXN109		1152	JXC460	
1011	JXN39	1082	JXN110		1153	JXC461	
1012	JXN40	1083	JXN111		1154	JXC462	
1013	JXN41	1084	JXN112		1155	JXC463	
1014	JXN42	1085	JXN113		1156	JXC464	
1015	JXN43	1086	JXN114		1157	JXC465	
1016	JXN44	1087	JXN115		1158	JXC466	
1017	JXN45	1088	JXN116		1159	JXC467	
1018	JXN46	1089	JXN117		1160	JXC468	
1019	JXN47	1090	JXN118		1161	JXC469	
1020	JXN48	1091	JXN119		1162	JXC470	
1021	JXN49	1092	JXN120		1163	JXC471	
1022	JXN50	1093	JXN121		1164	JXC472	
1023	JXN51	1094	JXN122		1165	JXC473	
1024	JXN52	1095	JXN123		1166	JXC474	
1025	JXN53	1096	JXN124		1167	JXC475	
1026	JXN54	1097	JXN125		1168	JXC476	
1027	JXN55	1098	JXN126		1169	JXC477	
1028	JXN56	1099	JXN127		1170	JXC478	
1029	JXN57	1100	JXN128		1171	JXC479	
1030	JXN58	1101	JXN129		1172	JXC480	
1031	JXN59	1102	JXN130		1173	JXC481	
1032	JXN60	1103	JXN131		1174	JXC482	
1033	JXN61	1104	JXN132		1175	JXC483	
1034	JXN62	1105	JXN133		1176	JXC484	
1035	JXN63	1106	JXN134		1177	JXC485	
1036	JXN64	1107	JXN135		1178	JXC486	
1037	JXN65	1108	JXN136		1179	JXC487	
1038	JXN66	1109	JXN137		1180	JXC488	1.2.58
1039	JXN67	1110	JXN138		1181	JXC489	
1040	JXN68	1111	JXN139		1182	KGK651	
1041	JXN69	1112	JXN140		1183	KGK652	
1042	JXN70	1113	JXN141		1184	KGK653	
1043	JXN71	1114	JXN142		1185	KGK654	
1044	JXN72	1115	JXN143		1186	KGK655	
1045	JXN73	1116	JXN144		1187	KGK656	
1046	JXN74	1117	JXN145		1188	KGK657	
1047	JXN75	1118	JXN146		1189	KGK658	
1048	JXN76	1119	JXN147		1190	KGK659	

RT		Date out of stock	RT		Date out of stock	RT		Date out of stock
1191	KGK660		1262	KLB511		1333	KLB582	
1192	KGK661		1263	KLB512		1334	KLB583	
1193	KGK662		1264	KLB513		1335	KLB584	
1194	KGK663		1265	KLB514		1336	KLB585	
1195	KGK664		1266	KLB515		1337	KLB586	
1196	KGK665		1267	KLB516		1338	KLB587	
1197	KGK666		1268	KLB517		1339	KLB588	
1198	KGK667		1269	KLB518		1340	KLB589	
1199	KGK668		1270	KLB519	27.2.58	1341	KLB590	
1200	KGK669		1271	KLB520		1342	KLB591	
1201	KGK670		1272	KLB521		1343	KLB592	
1202	KGK671		1273	KLB522		1344	KLB593	
1203	KGK672		1274	KLB523		1345	KLB594	
1204	KGK673		1275	KLB524		1346	KLB595	
1205	KGK674		1276	KLB525		1347	KLB596	
1206	KGK675		1277	KLB526	27.2.58	1348	KLB597	
1207	KGK676		1278	KLB527	27.2.58	1349	KLB598	
1208	KGK677		1279	KLB528		1350	KLB599	
1209	KGK678		1280	KLB529		1351	KLB600	
1210	KGK679		1281	KLB530	22.4.58	1352	KXW451	
1211	KGK680		1282	KLB531		1353	KXW452	
1212	KGK681		1283	KLB532		1354	KXW453	
1213	KGK682		1284	KLB533	27.2.58	1355	KXW454	
1214	KGK683		1285	KLB534		1356	KXW455	
1215	KGK684		1286	KLB535		1357	KXW456	
1216	KGK685		1287	KLB536		1358	KXW457	
1217	KGK686		1288	KLB537		1359	KXW458	
1218	KGK687	–	1289	KLB538		1360	KXW459	
1219	KGK688		1290	KLB539		1361	KXW460	
1220	KGK689		1291	KLB540	27.2.58	1362	KXW461	
1221	KGK690		1292	KLB541		1363	KXW462	
1222	KGK691		1293	KLB542		1364	KXW463	
1223	KGK692		1294	KLB543		1365	KXW464	
1224	KGK693		1295	KLB544		1366	KXW465	
1225	KGK694		1296	KLB545		1367	KXW466	
1226	KGK695		1297	KLB546		1368	KXW467	
1227	KGK696		1298	KLB547		1369	KXW468	
1228	KGK697		1299	KLB548		1370	KXW469	
1229	KGK698		1300	KLB549		1371	KXW470	
1230	KGK699		1301	KLB550		1372	KXW471	
1231	KGK700		1302	KLB551		1373	KXW472	
1232	KGK701	27.2.58	1303	KLB552		1374	KXW473	
1233	KGK702		1304	KLB553		1375	KXW474	
1234	KGK703		1305	KLB554		1376	KXW475	
1235	KGK704		1306	KLB555		1377	KXW476	
1236	KGK705		1307	KLB556	27.2.58	1378	KXW477	
1237	KGK706		1308	KLB557		1379	KXW478	
1238	KGK707		1309	KLB558		1380	KXW479	
1239	KGK708		1310	KLB559		1381	KXW480	
1240	KGK709		1311	KLB560		1382	KXW481	
1241	KGK710	27.2.58	1312	KLB561		1383	KXW482	
1242	KGK711		1313	KLB562		1384	KXW483	
1243	KGK712		1314	KLB563		1385	KXW484	
1244	KGK713		1315	KLB564	27.2.58	1386	KXW485	
1245	KGK714		1316	KLB565		1387	KXW486	
1246	KGK715		1317	KLB566		1388	KXW487	
1247	KGK716		1318	KLB567		1389	KXW488	
1248	KGK717		1319	KLB568		1390	KXW489	
1249	KGK718		1320	KLB569		1391	KXW490	
1250	KGK719		1321	KLB570		1392	KXW491	
1251	KGK720		1322	KLB571		1393	KXW492	
1252	KLB501		1323	KLB572		1394	KXW493	
1253	KLB502		1324	KLB573		1395	KXW494	
1254	KLB503		1325	KLB574		1396	KXW495	
1255	KLB504		1326	KLB575		1397	KXW496	
1256	KLB505		1327	KLB576		1398	KXW497	
1257	KLB506		1328	KLB577		1399	KXW498	
1258	KLB507		1329	KLB578		1400	KXW499	
1259	KLB508		1330	KLB579		1401	KXW500	
1260	KLB509		1331	KLB580		1402	JXC165	15.1.57
1261	KLB510		1332	KLB581		1403	JXC166	1.9.56

RT		Date out of stock	RT		Date out of stock	RT		Date out of stock
1404	JXC167	5.2.57	1475	KGK734	23.8.56	1546	KGU415	
1405	JXC168	15.5. 56	1476	KGK735	10.8.56	1547	KGU416	
1406	JXC169	19.5.56	1477	KGK736	22.10.56	1548	KGU440	
1407	JXC170	14.5.56	1478	KGK737	17.7.56	1549	KGU441	
1408	JXC171	3.5.56	1479	KGK738	18.1.57	1550	KGU442	
1409	JXC172	19.5.56	1480	KGK739	25.4.56	1551	KGU443	
1410	JXC173	6.7.56	1481	KGK740	7.9.56	1552	KGU444	
1411	JXC174	3.5.56	1482	KGK741	15.1.57	1553	KGU445	
1412	JXC175	5.7.56	1483	KGK742	10.8.56	1554	KGU446	
1413	JXC176	14.5.56	1484	KGK743	1.5.57	1555	KGU447	
1414	JXC177	3.5.56	1485	KGK744	10.8.56	1556	KGU448	
1415	JXC178	11.5.56	1486	KGK745	11.4.57	1557	KGU449	
1416	JXC179	11.5.56	1487	KGK746	10.8.56	1558	KGU450	
1417	JXC180	19.5.56	1488	KGK747	22.10.56	1559	KLB631	
1418	JXC181	19.5.56	1489	KGK748	30.4.57	1560	KLB632	
1419	JXC182	6.7.56	1490	KGK749	30.4.57	1561	KLB633	
1420	JXC183	s 21.6.56	1491	KGK750	22.10.56	1562	KLB634	
1421	JXC184	6.7.56	1492	KGK751	16.8.56	1563	KLB635	
1422	JXC185	6.7.56	1493	KGK752	10.8.56	1564	KLB636	
1423	JXC186	5.7.56	1494	KGK753	22.6.56	1565	KLB637	
1424	JXC187	29.6.56	1495	KGK754	16.10.56	1566	KLB638	
1425	JXC188	11.5.56	1496	KGK755	16.10.56	1567	KLB655	
1426	JXC189	11.6.56	1497	KGK756	16.10.56	1568	KLB656	
1427	JXC190	19.5.56	1498	KGK757	1.5.57	1569	KLB657	
1428	JXC191	2.7.56	1499	KGK758	11.4.57	1570	KLB658	
1429	JXC192	17.5.56	1500	KGK759	30.4.57	1571	KLB659	
1430	JXC193	22.6.56	1501	KGK760	30.4.57	1572	KLB660	
1431	JXC194	30.4.56	1502	KGK761	10.8.56	1573	KLB661	
1432	JXC195	22.6.56	1503	KGK762	10.8.56	1574	KLB662	
1433	JXC196	5.7.56	1504	KGK763	30.4.57	1575	KLB663	
1434	JXC197	6.7.56	1505	KGK764	29.6.56	1576	KLB664	
1435	JXC198	29.6.56	1506	KGK765	11.4.57	1577	KLB665	
1436	JXC199	11.5.56	1507	KGK766	10.8.56	1578	KLB666	
1437	JXC200	22.6.56	1508	KGK767	30.4.57	1579	KLB667	
1438	JXC201	11.5.56	1509	KGK768	1.5.57	1580	KLB668	
1439	JXC202	22.6.56	1510	KGK769	30.10.56	1581	KLB669	
1440	JXC203	29.6.56	1511	KGK770	30.4.56	1582	KLB670	
1441	JXC204	2.7.56	1512	KGK771	30.4.56	1583	KLB671	
1442	JXC205	11.6.56	1513	KGK772	30.4.56	1584	KLB672	
1443	JXC206	26.4.56	1514	KGK773	16.8.56	1585	KLB673	
1444	JXC207	3.5.56	1515	KGK774	10.8.56	1586	KLB674	
1445	JXC208	8.5.56	1516	KGK775	1.5.57	1587	KLB675	
1446	JXC209	30.4.56	1517	KGK776	30.4.57	1588	KLB676	
1447	JXC210	17.5.56	1518	KGK777	20.8.56	1589	KLB677	
1448	JXC211	11.5.56	1519	KGK778	23.8.56	1590	KLB678	
1449	JXC212	22.6.56	1520	KGK779	17.7.56	1591	KLB713	
1450	JXC213	5.7.56	1521	KGK780	10.8.56	1592	KLB714	
1451	JXC214	29.6.56	1522	KGU236		1593	KLB715	
1452	JXC215	4.5.56	1523	KGU237		1594	KLB716	
1453	JXC216	19.5.56	1524	KGU238		1595	KLB717	
1454	JXC217	5.7.56	1525	KGU239		1596	KLB718	
1455	JXC218	5.7.56	1526	KGU240		1597	KLB719	
1456	JXC219	25.4.56	1527	KGU241		1598	KLB720	
1457	JXC220	30.4.57	1528	KGU242		1599	KLB721	
1458	JXC221	22.6.56	1529	KGU243		1600	KLB722	
1459	JXC222	10.8.56	1530	KGU290		1601	KLB723	
1460	JXC223	10.8.56	1531	KGU291		1602	KLB724	
1461	JXC224	5.2.57	1532	KGU292		1603	KLB725	
1462	KGK721	15.1.57	1533	KGU293		1604	KLB726	
1463	KGK722	10.8.56	1534	KGU294		1605	KLB727	27.2.58
1464	KGK723	7.9.56	1535	KGU295		1606	KLB728	
1465	KGK724	15.1.57	1536	KGU296		1607	KLB729	
1466	KGK725	15.1.57	1537	KGU297		1608	KLB730	
1467	KGK726	1.9.56	1538	KGU298		1609	KLB731	
1468	KGK727	15.5. 56	1539	KGU299		1610	KLB732	
1469	KGK728	10.8.56	1540	KGU300		1611	KLB733	
1470	KGK729	18.1.57	1541	KGU410		1612	KLB734	
1471	KGK730	6.7.56	1542	KGU411		1613	KLB735	
1472	KGK731	22.10.56	1543	KGU412		1614	KLB736	
1473	KGK732	10.8.56	1544	KGU413		1615	KLB737	
1474	KGK733	10.8.56	1545	KGU414		1616	KLB738	

RT		Date out of stock	RT		Date out of stock	RT	
1617	KLB739		1688	KXW334		1759	KYY597
1618	KLB740		1689	KXW335		1760	KYY598
1619	KLB741		1690	KXW336		1761	KYY599
1620	KLB742		1691	KXW337		1762	KYY600
1621	KLB743		1692	KXW338		1763	KYY601
1622	KLB744		1693	KXW339	22.4.58	1764	KYY602
1623	KLB745		1694	KXW340		1765	KYY603
1624	KLB746		1695	KXW341		1766	KYY604
1625	KLB747		1696	KXW342		1767	KYY605
1626	KLB748		1697	KXW343		1768	KYY606
1627	KLB749		1698	KYY525	27.2.58	1769	KYY607
1628	KLB750		1699	KYY526		1770	KYY608
1629	KXW251		1700	KYY527		1771	KYY609
1630	KXW252		1701	KYY528		1772	KYY610
1631	KXW253		1702	KYY529		1773	KYY611
1632	KXW254		1703	KYY530		1774	KYY612
1633	KXW255		1704	KYY531		1775	KYY613
1634	KXW256		1705	KYY532		1776	KYY614
1635	KXW257		1706	KYY533		1777	KYY615
1636	KXW258		1707	KYY534	27.2.58	1778	KYY616
1637	KXW259		1708	KYY535		1779	KYY617
1638	KXW260		1709	KYY536		1780	KYY618
1639	KXW261		1710	KYY537		1781	KYY619
1640	KXW262		1711	KYY538		1782	KYY620
1641	KXW263		1712	KYY539		1783	KYY621
1642	KXW264		1713	KYY540		1784	KYY622
1643	KXW265		1714	KYY541	27.2.58	1785	KYY623
1644	KXW266		1715	KYY542		1786	KYY624
1645	KXW267		1716	KYY543		1787	KYY625
1646	KXW268		1717	KYY544		1788	KYY626
1647	KXW269		1718	KYY545		1789	KYY627
1648	KXW270		1719	KYY546		1790	KYY628
1649	KXW271		1720	KYY547		1791	KYY629
1650	KXW272		1721	KYY548		1792	KYY630
1651	KXW273		1722	KYY549		1793	KYY631
1652	KXW274		1723	KYY550		1794	KYY632
1653	KXW275	27.2.58	1724	KYY551		1795	KYY650
1654	KXW276		1725	KYY552	27.2.58	1796	KYY651
1655	KXW301		1726	KYY553	22.4.58	1797	KYY652
1656	KXW302		1727	KYY554		1798	KYY653
1657	KXW303	27.2.58	1728	KYY555		1799	KYY654
1658	KXW304		1729	KYY556		1800	KYY655
1659	KXW305		1730	KYY557		1801	KYY656
1660	KXW306		1731	KYY569		1802	KYY657
1661	KXW307		1732	KYY570		1803	KYY658
1662	KXW308		1733	KYY571		1804	KYY659
1663	KXW309	27.2.58	1734	KYY572		1805	KYY660
1664	KXW310	22.4.58	1735	KYY573		1806	KYY661
1665	KXW311		1736	KYY574	27.2.58	1807	KYY662
1666	KXW312		1737	KYY575		1808	KYY663
1667	KXW313		1738	KYY576		1809	KYY664
1668	KXW314		1739	KYY577		1810	KYY665
1669	KXW315		1740	KYY578		1811	KYY666
1670	KXW316		1741	KYY579		1812	KYY667
1671	KXW317		1742	KYY580	27.2.58	1813	KYY668
1672	KXW318		1743	KYY581		1814	KYY669
1673	KXW319	22.4.58	1744	KYY582		1815	KYY670
1674	KXW320		1745	KYY583		1816	KYY671
1675	KXW321	27.2.58	1746	KYY584		1817	KYY672
1676	KXW322		1747	KYY585		1818	KYY673
1677	KXW323		1748	KYY586		1819	KYY674
1678	KXW324		1749	KYY587		1820	KYY675
1679	KXW325		1750	KYY588		1821	KYY676
1680	KXW326	27.2.58	1751	KYY589		1822	KYY677
1681	KXW327		1752	KYY590		1823	KYY678
1682	KXW328		1753	KYY591		1824	KYY679
1683	KXW329		1754	KYY592		1825	KYY680
1684	KXW330		1755	KYY593		1826	KYY681
1685	KXW331		1756	KYY594		1827	KYY682
1686	KXW332		1757	KYY595	22.4.58	1828	KYY683
1687	KXW333		1758	KYY596		1829	KYY684

RT

RT

RT

1830	KYY685
1831	KYY686
1832	KYY687
1833	KYY688
1834	KYY689
1835	KYY690
1836	KYY691
1837	KYY692
1838	KYY693
1839	KYY694
1840	KYY695
1841	KYY696
1842	KYY697
1843	KYY698
1844	KYY699
1845	KYY700
1846	KYY701
1847	KYY702
1848	KYY703
1849	KYY704
1850	KYY716
1851	KYY717
1852	KYY718
1853	KYY719
1854	KYY720
1855	LLU741
1856	LLU742
1857	LLU743
1858	LLU744
1859	LLU745
1860	LLU746
1861	LLU747
1862	LLU748
1863	LLU749
1864	LLU750
1865	LLU751
1866	LLU752
1867	LLU753
1868	LLU754
1869	LLU755
1870	LLU756
1871	LLU757
1872	LLU758
1873	LLU759
1874	LLU760
1875	LLU761
1876	LLU762
1877	LLU763
1878	LLU764
1879	LLU765
1880	LLU766
1881	LLU767
1882	LLU768
1883	LLU769
1884	LLU770
1885	LLU771
1886	LLU794
1887	LLU795
1888	LLU796
1889	LLU797
1890	LLU798
1891	LLU799
1892	LLU800
1893	LLU801
1894	LLU802
1895	LLU803
1896	LLU804
1897	LLU805
1898	LLU806
1899	LLU807
1900	LLU808

1901	LLU809
1902	LLU810
1903	LLU811
1904	LLU812
1905	LLU813
1906	LLU814
1907	LLU815
1908	LLU816
1909	LLU817
1910	LLU818
1911	LLU831
1912	LLU832
1913	LLU833
1914	LLU834
1915	LLU835
1916	LLU836
1917	LLU837
1918	LLU838
1919	LLU839
1920	LLU840
1921	LUC1
1922	LUC2
1923	LUC3
1924	LUC4
1925	LUC5
1926	LUC6
1927	LUC7
1928	LUC8
1929	LUC9
1930	LUC10
1931	LUC11
1932	LUC12
1933	LUC13
1934	LUC14
1935	LUC15
1936	LUC16
1937	LUC17
1938	LUC18
1939	LUC19
1940	LUC20
1941	LUC21
1942	LUC22
1943	LUC29
1944	LUC30
1945	LUC31
1946	LUC32
1947	LUC33
1948	LUC34
1949	LUC35
1950	LUC36
1951	LUC37
1952	LUC38
1953	LUC39
1954	LUC40
1955	LUC44
1956	LUC45
1957	LUC46
1958	LUC47
1959	LUC48
1960	LUC49
1961	LUC50
1962	LUC51
1963	LUC52
1964	LUC53
1965	LUC54
1966	LUC55
1967	LUC56
1968	LUC57
1969	LUC58
1970	LUC59
1971	LUC60

1972	LUC61
1973	LUC62
1974	LUC63
1975	LUC64
1976	LUC65
1977	LUC66
1978	LUC67
1979	LUC80
1980	LUC81
1981	LUC82
1982	LUC83
1983	LUC84
1984	LUC85
1985	LUC86
1986	LUC87
1987	LUC88
1988	LUC89
1989	LUC90
1990	LUC91
1991	LUC92
1992	LUC93
1993	LUC94
1994	LUC95
1995	LUC96
1996	LUC97
1997	LUC98
1998	LUC99
1999	LUC100
2000	LUC226
2001	LUC227
2002	LUC228
2003	LUC229
2004	LUC230
2005	LUC231
2006	LUC232
2007	LUC233
2008	LUC234
2009	LUC235
2010	LUC236
2011	LUC237
2012	LUC238
2013	LUC239
2014	LUC240
2015	LUC241
2016	LUC242
2017	LUC243
2018	LUC244
2019	LUC245
2020	LUC246
2021	LUC247
2022	LUC248
2023	LUC249
2024	LUC266
2025	LUC267
2026	LUC268
2027	LUC269
2028	LUC270
2029	LUC271
2030	LUC272
2031	LUC273
2032	LUC274
2033	LUC275
2034	LUC276
2035	LUC277
2036	LUC278
2037	LUC279
2038	LUC280
2039	LUC281
2040	LUC288
2041	LUC289
2042	LUC290

RT

2043	LUC291	2114	LYF169	2185	KGU114
2044	LUC292	2115	LYF170	2186	KGU115
2045	LUC293	2116	KLB981	2187	KGU116
2046	LUC294	2117	KLB982	2188	KGU117
2047	LUC295	2118	KLB983	2189	KGU118
2048	LUC296	2119	KLB984	2190	KGU119
2049	LUC297	2120	KLB985	2191	KGU120
2050	LUC298	2121	KLB986	2192	KGU121
2051	LUC299	2122	KGK931	2193	KGU122
2052	LUC300	2123	KGK932	2194	KGU123
2053	LUC301	2124	KGK933	2195	KGU124
2054	LUC302	2125	KGK934	2196	KGU125
2055	LUC303	2126	KGK935	2197	KGU126
2056	LUC304	2127	KGK936	2198	KGU127
2057	LUC320	2128	KGK937	2199	KGU128
2058	LUC321	2129	KGK938	2200	KGU129
2059	LUC322	2130	KGK939	2201	KGU130
2060	LUC323	2131	KGK940	2202	KGU131
2061	LUC324	2132	KGK941	2203	KGU132
2062	LUC325	2133	KGK942	2204	KGU133
2063	LYF1	2134	KGK943	2205	KGU134
2064	LYF2	2135	KGK944	2206	KGU135
2065	LYF3	2136	KGK945	2207	KGU136
2066	LYF4.	2137	KGK946	2208	KGU137
2067	LYF5	2138	KGK947	2209	KGU138
2068	LYF6	2139	KGK948	2210	KGU139
2069	LYF7	2140	KGK949	2211	KGU140
2070	LYF8	2141	KGK950	2212	KGU141
2071	LYF9	2142	KGK951	2213	KGU142
2072	LYF10	2143	KGK952	2214	KGU143
2073	LYF11	2144	KGK953	2215	KGU144
2074	LYF12	2145	KGK954	2216	KGU145
2075	LYF13	2146	KGK955	2217	KGU146
2076	LYF14	2147	KGK956	2218	KGU147
2077	LYF15	2148	KGK957	2219	KGU148
2078	LYF16	2149	KGK958	2220	KGU149
2079	LYF17	2150	KGK959	2221	KGU150
2080	LYF18	2151	KGK960	2222	KGU151
2081	LYF19	2152	KGK961	2223	KGU152
2082	LYF20	2153	KGK962	2224	KGU153
2083	LYF21	2154	KGK963	2225	KGU154
2084	LYF22	2155	KGK964	2226	KGU155
2085	LYF23	2156	KGK965	2227	KGU156
2086	LYF24	2157	KGK966	2228	KGU157
2087	LYF25	2158	KGK967	2229	KGU158
2088	LYF26	2159	KGK968	2230	KGU159
2089	LYF27	2160	KGK969	2231	KGU160
2090	LYF28	2161	KGK970	2232	KGU161
2091	LYF29	2162	KGK971	2233	KGU162
2092	LYF30	2163	KGK972	2234	KGU163
2093	LYF31	2164	KGK973	2235	KGU164
2094	LYF32	2165	KGK974	2236	KGU165
2095	LYF33	2166	KGK975	2237	KGU166
2096	LYF72	2167	KGK976	2238	KGU167
2097	LYF73	2168	KGK977	2239	KGU168
2098	LYF74	2169	KGK978	2240	KGU169
2099	LYF75	2170	KGK979	2241	KGU170
2100	LYF76	2171	KGK980	2242	KGU171
2101	LYF77	2172	KGU101	2243	KGU172
2102	LYF78	2173	KGU102	2244	KGU173
2103	LYF79	2174	KGU103	2245	KGU174
2104	LYF80	2175	KGU104	2246	KGU175
2105	LYF81	2176	KGU105	2247	KGU176
2106	LYF82	2177	KGU106	2248	KGU177
2107	LYF83	2178	KGU107	2249	KGU178
2108	LYF84	2179	KGU108	2250	KGU179
2109	LYF85	2180	KGU109	2251	KGU180
2110	LYF86	2181	KGU110	2252	KGU181
2111	LYF87	2182	KGU111	2253	KGU182
2112	LYF88	2183	KGU112	2254	KGU183
2113	LYF168	2184	KGU113	2255	KGU184

RT		Date out of stock	RT		Date out of stock	RT		Date out of stock
2256	KGU185		2327	KGU356		2398	KLB777	
2257	KGU186		2328	KGU357		2399	KLB778	
2258	KGU187		2329	KGU358		2400	KLB779	
2259	KGU188		2330	KGU359		2401	KLB780	
2260	KGU189		2331	KGU360		2402	KLB781	
2261	KGU190		2332	KGU361		2403	KLB782	
2262	KGU191		2333	KGU362		2404	KLB783	
2263	KGU192		2334	KGU363		2405	KLB784	
2264	KGU193		2335	KGU364		2406	KLB785	
2265	KGU194		2336	KGU365		2407	KLB786	
2266	KGU195		2337	KGU366		2408	KLB787	
2267	KGU196		2338	KGU367		2409	KLB788	
2268	KGU197		2339	KGU368		2410	KLB789	
2269	KGU198		2340	KGU369		2411	KLB790	
2270	KGU199		2341	KGU370		2412	KLB791	
2271	KGU200		2342	KGU371		2413	KLB792	
2272	KGU301		2343	KGU372		2414	KLB793	
2273	KGU302		2344	KGU373		2415	KLB794	
2274	KGU303		2345	KGU374		2416	KLB795	
2275	KGU304		2346	KGU375		2417	KLB796	
2276	KGU305		2347	KGU376		2418	KLB797	
2277	KGU306		2348	KGU377		2419	KLB798	
2278	KGU307		2349	KGU378		2420	KLB799	
2279	KGU308		2350	KGU379		2421	KLB800	
2280	KGU309		2351	KGU380		2422	KLB801	
2281	KGU310		2352	KGU381		2423	KLB802	
2282	KGU311		2353	KGU382		2424	KLB803	27.2.58
2283	KGU312		2354	KGU383		2425	KLB804	
2284	KGU313		2355	KGU384		2426	KLB805	
2285	KGU314		2356	KGU385		2427	KLB806	
2286	KGU315		2357	KGU386		2428	KLB807	
2287	KGU316		2358	KGU387		2429	KLB808	
2288	KGU317		2359	KGU388		2430	KLB809	
2289	KGU318		2360	KGU389		2431	KLB810	
2290	KGU319		2361	KGU390		2432	KLB811	
2291	KGU320		2362	KGU391		2433	KLB812	
2292	KGU321		2363	KGU392		2434	KLB813	
2293	KGU322		2364	KGU393		2435	KLB814	
2294	KGU323		2365	KGU394		2436	KLB815	
2295	KGU324		2366	KGU395	19.4.62	2437	KLB816	
2296	KGU325		2367	KGU396		2438	KLB817	
2297	KGU326		2368	KGU397		2439	KLB818	
2298	KGU327		2369	KGU398		2440	KLB819	
2299	KGU328		2370	KGU399		2441	KLB820	
2300	KGU329		2371	KGU400		2442	KLB821	
2301	KGU330		2372	KLB751		2443	KLB822	
2302	KGU331		2373	KLB752		2444	KLB823	
2303	KGU332		2374	KLB753		2445	KLB824	
2304	KGU333		2375	KLB754		2446	KLB825	
2305	KGU334	19.4.62	2376	KLB755		2447	KLB826	
2306	KGU335		2377	KLB756		2448	KLB827	
2307	KGU336		2378	KLB757		2449	KLB828	
2308	KGU337		2379	KLB758		2450	KLB829	
2309	KGU338		2380	KLB759		2451	KLB830	
2310	KGU339		2381	KLB760		2452	KLB831	
2311	KGU340		2382	KLB761		2453	KLB832	
2312	KGU341		2383	KLB762		2454	KLB833	
2313	KGU342		2384	KLB763		2455	KLB834	
2314	KGU343		2385	KLB764		2456	KLB835	
2315	KGU344		2386	KLB765		2457	KLB836	
2316	KGU345		2387	KLB766		2458	KLB837	
2317	KGU346		2388	KLB767		2459	KLB838	
2318	KGU347		2389	KLB768		2460	KLB839	
2319	KGU348		2390	KLB769		2461	KLB840	
2320	KGU349		2391	KLB770		2462	KLB841	
2321	KGU350		2392	KLB771		2463	KLB842	
2322	KGU351		2393	KLB772		2464	KLB843	
2323	KGU352		2394	KLB773		2465	KLB844	
2324	KGU353		2395	KLB774		2466	KLB845	
2325	KGU354		2396	KLB775		2467	KLB846	
2326	KGU355		2397	KLB776		2468	KLB847	

RT

RT		Date out of stock	RT		RT	
2469	KLB848		2540	LYF189	2611	LYF336
2470	KLB849		2541	LYF190	2612	LYF337
2471	KLB850		2542	LYF191	2613	LYF338
2472	KXW101		2543	LYF192	2614	LYF339
2473	KXW102		2544	LYF193	2615	LYF340
2474	KXW103		2545	LYF194	2616	LYF341
2475	KXW104		2546	LYF195	2617	LYF342
2476	KXW105		2547	LYF196	2618	LYF343
2477	KXW106		2548	LYF197	2619	LYF344
2478	KXW107		2549	LYF198	2620	LYF345
2479	KXW108		2550	LYF199	2621	LYF346
2480	KXW109		2551	LYF200	2622	LYF347
2481	KXW110		2552	LYF277	2623	LYF348
2482	KXW111		2553	LYF278	2624	LYF349
2483	KXW112		2554	LYF279	2625	LYF350
2484	KXW113		2555	LYF280	2626	LYF351
2485	KXW114		2556	LYF281	2627	LYF352
2486	KXW115		2557	LYF282	2628	LYF353
2487	KXW116		2558	LYF283	2629	LYF354
2488	KXW117		2559	LYF284	2630	LYF355
2489	KXW118		2560	LYF285	2631	LYF356
2490	KXW119		2561	LYF286	2632	LYF357
2491	KXW120		2562	LYF287	2633	LYF358
2492	KXW121		2563	LYF288	2634	LYF359
2493	KXW122		2564	LYF289	2635	LYF360
2494	KXW123		2565	LYF290	2636	LYF361
2495	KXW124		2566	LYF291	2637	LYF362
2496	KXW125	7.9.62	2567	LYF292	2638	LYF363
2497	KXW126		2568	LYF293	2639	LYF364
2498	KXW127		2569	LYF294	2640	LYF365
2499	KXW128		2570	LYF295	2641	LYF366
2500	KXW129		2571	LYF296	2642	LYF367
2501	KXW130		2572	LYF297	2643	LYF368
2502	KXW131		2573	LYF298	2644	LYF369
2503	KXW132		2574	LYF299	2645	LYF370
2504	KXW133		2575	LYF300	2646	LYF371
2505	KXW134		2576	LYF301	2647	LYF372
2506	KXW135		2577	LYF302	2648	LYF373
2507	KXW136		2578	LYF303	2649	LYF374
2508	KXW137		2579	LYF304	2650	LYF375
2509	KXW138		2580	LYF305	2651	LYF376
2510	KXW139		2581	LYF306	2652	LYR636
2511	KXW140		2582	LYF307	2653	LYR637
2512	KXW141		2583	LYF308	2654	LYR638
2513	KXW142		2584	LYF309	2655	LYR639
2514	KXW143		2585	LYF310	2656	LYR640
2515	KXW144		2586	LYF311	2657	LYR641
2516	KXW145		2587	LYF312	2658	LYR642
2517	KXW146		2588	LYF313	2659	LYR643
2518	KXW147		2589	LYF314	2660	LYR644
2519	KXW148		2590	LYF315	2661	LYR645
2520	KXW149		2591	LYF316	2662	LYR646
2521	KXW150		2592	LYF317	2663	LYR647
2522	LYF171		2593	LYF318	2664	LYR648
2523	LYF172		2594	LYF319	2665	LYR649
2524	LYF173		2595	LYF320	2666	LYR650
2525	LYF174		2596	LYF321	2667	LYR651
2526	LYF175		2597	LYF322	2668	LYR652
2527	LYF176		2598	LYF323	2669	LYR653
2528	LYF177		2599	LYF324	2670	LYR654
2529	LYF178		2600	LYF325	2671	LYR655
2530	LYF179		2601	LYF326	2672	LYR656
2531	LYF180		2602	LYF327	2673	LYR657
2532	LYF181		2603	LYF328	2674	LYR658
2533	LYF182		2604	LYF329	2675	LYR659
2534	LYF183		2605	LYF330	2676	LYR660
2535	LYF184		2606	LYF331	2677	LYR661
2536	LYF185		2607	LYF332	2678	LYR662
2537	LYF186		2608	LYF333	2679	LYR663
2538	LYF187		2609	LYF334	2680	LYR664
2539	LYF188		2610	LYF335	2681	LYR665

RT

2682	LYR666
2683	LYR667
2684	LYR668
2685	LYR669
2686	LYR670
2687	LYR671
2688	LYR672
2689	LYR673
2690	LYR674
2691	LYR675
2692	LYR676
2693	LYR677
2694	LYR678
2695	LYR679
2696	LYR680
2697	LYR681
2698	LYR682
2699	LYR683
2700	LYR684
2701	LYR685
2702	LYR686
2703	LYR687
2704	LYR688
2705	LYR689
2706	LYR690
2707	LYR691
2708	LYR692
2709	LYR693
2710	LYR694
2711	LYR695
2712	LYR696
2713	LYR697
2714	LYR698
2715	LYR699
2716	LYR700
2717	LYR701
2718	LYR702
2719	LYR703
2720	LYR704
2721	LYR705
2722	LYR706
2723	LYR707
2724	LYR708
2725	LYR709
2726	LYR710
2727	LYR711
2728	LYR712
2729	LYR713
2730	LYR714
2731	LYR715
2732	LYR716
2733	LYR717
2734	LYR718
2735	LYR719
2736	LYR720
2737	LYR721
2738	LYR722
2739	LYR723
2740	LYR724
2741	LYR725
2742	LYR726
2743	LYR727
2744	LYR728
2745	LYR729
2746	LYR730
2747	LYR731
2748	LYR732
2749	LYR733
2750	LYR734
2751	LYR735
2752	LYR736

RT

2753	LYR737
2754	LYR738
2755	LYR739
2756	LYR740
2757	LYR741
2758	LYR742
2759	LYR743
2760	LYR744
2761	LYR745
2762	LYR746
2763	LYR747
2764	LYR748
2765	LYR749
2766	LYR750
2767	LYR751
2768	LYR752
2769	LYR753
2770	LYR754
2771	LYR755
2772	LYR756
2773	LYR757
2774	LYR758
2775	LYR826
2776	LYR827
2777	LYR941
2778	LYR942
2779	LYR943
2780	LYR944
2781	LYR945
2782	LYR946
2783	LYR947
2784	LYR948
2785	LYR949
2786	LYR950
2787	LYR951
2788	LYR952
2789	LYR953
2790	LYR954
2791	LYR955
2792	LYR962
2793	LYR963
2794	LYR964
2795	LYR965
2796	LYR966
2797	LYR967
2798	LYR968
2799	LYR969
2800	LYR970
2801	LYR971
2802	LYR972
2803	LYR973
2804	LYR974
2805	LYR975
2806	LYR976
2807	LYR977
2808	LYR978
2809	LYR979
2810	LYR980
2811	LYR981
2812	LYR982
2813	LYR983
2814	LYR984
2815	LYR985
2816	LYR986
2817	LYR987
2818	LYR988
2819	LYR989
2820	LYR990
2821	LYR991
2822	LYR992
2823	LYR993

RT

2824	LYR994
2825	LYR995
2826	LYR996
2827	LYR997
2828	LYR998
2829	LYR999
2830	LYF477
2831	LYF478
2832	LYF479
2833	LYF480
2834	LYF481
2835	LYF482
2836	LYF483
2837	LYF484
2838	LYF485
2839	LYF486
2840	LYF487
2841	LYF488
2842	LYF489
2843	LYF490
2844	LYF491
2845	LYF492
2846	LYF493
2847	LYF494
2848	LYF495
2849	LYF496
2850	LYF497
2851	LYF498
2852	LYF499
2853	LYF500
2854	MLL501
2855	MLL502
2856	MLL503
2857	MLL504
2858	MLL505
2859	MLL506
2860	MLL507
2861	MLL508
2862	MLL509
2863	MLL510
2864	MLL511
2865	MLL512
2866	MLL613
2867	MLL614
2868	MLL615
2869	MLL616
2870	MLL617
2871	MLL618
2872	MLL619
2873	MLL620
2874	MLL621
2875	MLL622
2876	MLL623
2877	MLL624
2878	MLL625
2879	MLL626
2880	MLL627
2881	MLL628
2882	MLL629
2883	MLL630
2884	MLL631
2885	MLL632
2886	MLL633
2887	MLL634
2888	MLL635
2889	MLL636
2890	MLL637
2891	MLL638
2892	MLL639
2893	MLL640
2894	MLL641

RT

RT		RT		RT		Date out of stock
2895	MLL642	2966	MXX55	3037	NLE927	
2896	MLL643	2967	MXX56	3038	NLE928	
2897	MLL644	2968	MXX57	3039	NLE929	
2898	MLL645	2969	MXX58	3040	NLE930	
2899	MLL646	2970	MXX59	3041	NLE931	
2900	MLL647	2971	MXX60	3042	KXW151	
2901	MLL648	2972	NLE740	3043	KXW152	
2902	MLL649	2973	NLE741	3044	KXW153	
2903	MLL650	2974	NLE742	3045	KXW154	
2904	MLL651	2975	NLE743	3046	KXW155	
2905	MLL652	2976	NLE744	3047	KXW156	
2906	MLL653	2977	NLE745	3048	KXW157	
2907	MLL654	2978	NLE746	3049	KXW158	
2908	MLL655	2979	NLE747	3050	KXW159	
2909	MLL656	2980	NLE748	3051	KXW160	
2910	MLL657	2981	NLE749	3052	KXW161	
2911	MLL658	2982	NLE750	3053	KXW162	
2912	MLL659	2983	NLE754	3054	KXW163	
2913	MLL660	2984	NLE755	3055	KXW164	
2914	MLL661	2985	NLE756	3056	KXW165	
2915	MLL662	2986	NLE757	3057	KXW166	22.4.58
2916	MLL663	2987	NLE758	3058	KXW167	
2917	MLL664	2988	NLE759	3059	KXW168	
2918	MLL665	2989	NLE760	3060	KXW169	
2919	MLL666	2990	NLE761	3061	KXW170	
2920	MLL667	2991	NLE762	3062	KXW171	
2921	MLL668	2992	NLE763	3063	KXW172	
2922	MLL669	2993	NLE764	3064	KXW173	
2923	MLL670	2994	NLE765	3065	KXW174	
2924	MLL671	2995	NLE766	3066	KXW175	
2925	MLL672	2996	NLE767	3067	KXW176	
2926	MLL673	2997	NLE768	3068	KXW177	
2927	MLL674	2998	NLE769	3069	KXW178	
2928	MLL675	2999	NLE770	3070	KXW179	
2929	MLL688	3000	NLE771	3071	KXW180	
2930	MLL689	3001	NLE772	3072	KXW181	
2931	MLL690	3002	NLE773	3073	KXW182	27.2.58
2932	MLL691	3003	NLE774	3074	KXW183	
2933	MLL692	3004	NLE775	3075	KXW184	27.2.58
2934	MLL693	3005	NLE776	3076	KXW185	27.2.58
2935	MLL694	3006	NLE777	3077	KXW186	
2936	MLL695	3007	NLE778	3078	KXW187	
2937	MLL696	3008	NLE779	3079	KXW188	
2938	MLL704	3009	NLE780	3080	KXW189	
2939	MLL705	3010	NLE781	3081	KXW190	
2940	MLL706	3011	NLE901	3082	KXW191	27.2.58
2941	MLL707	3012	NLE902	3083	KXW192	
2942	MLL708	3013	NLE903	3084	KXW193	
2943	MLL709	3014	NLE904	3085	KXW194	
2944	MLL710	3015	NLE905	3086	KXW195	
2945	MLL711	3016	NLE906	3087	KXW196	
2946	MLL712	3017	NLE907	3088	KXW197	
2947	MXX31	3018	NLE908	3089	KXW198	
2948	MXX36	3019	NLE909	3090	KXW199	27.2.58
2949	MXX37	3020	NLE910	3091	KXW200	
2950	MXX38	3021	NLE911	3092	KXW201	
2951	MXX39	3022	NLE912	3093	KXW202	
2952	MXX41	3023	NLE913	3094	KXW203	
2953	MXX42	3024	NLE914	3095	KXW204	
2954	MXX43	3025	NLE915	3096	KXW205	
2955	MXX44	3026	NLE916	3097	KXW206	
2956	MXX45	3027	NLE917	3098	KXW207	
2957	MXX46	3028	NLE918	3099	KXW208	
2958	MXX47	3029	NLE919	3100	KXW209	
2959	MXX48	3030	NLE920	3101	KXW210	
2960	MXX49	3031	NLE921	3102	KXW211	
2961	MXX50	3032	NLE922	3103	KXW212	
2962	MXX51	3033	NLE923	3104	KXW213	
2963	MXX52	3034	NLE924	3105	KXW214	27.2.58
2964	MXX53	3035	NLE925	3106	KXW215	
2965	MXX54	3036	NLE926	3107	KXW216	

RT

RT		RT		RT		RT		RT	
3108	KXW217	3178	KYY907	3248	LLU607	3318	LYR537	3388	LYR607
3109	KXW218	3179	KYY908	3249	LLU608	3319	LYR538	3389	LYR608
3110	KXW219	3180	KYY909	3250	LLU609	3320	LYR539	3390	LYR609
3111	KXW220	3181	KYY910	3251	LLU610	3321	LYR540	3391	LYR610
3112	KXW221	3182	KYY911	3252	LLU611	3322	LYR541	3392	LYR611
3113	KXW222	3183	KYY912	3253	LLU612	3323	LYR542	3393	LYR612
3114	KXW223	3184	KYY913	3254	LLU613	3324	LYR543	3394	LYR613
3115	KXW224	3185	KYY914	3255	LLU614	3325	LYR544	3395	LYR614
3116	KXW225	3186	KYY915	3256	LLU615	3326	LYR545	3396	LYR615
3117	KXW226	3187	KYY916	3257	LLU616	3327	LYR546	3397	LYR616
3118	KXW227	3188	KYY917	3258	LLU617	3328	LYR547	3398	LYR617
3119	KXW228	3189	KYY918	3259	LLU618	3329	LYR548	3399	LYR618
3120	KXW229	3190	KYY919	3260	LLU619	3330	LYR549	3400	LYR619
3121	KXW230	3191	KYY920	3261	LLU620	3331	LYR550	3401	LYR620
3122	KXW231	3192	KYY921	3262	LLU621	3332	LYR551	3402	LYR621
3123	KXW232	3193	KYY922	3263	LLU622	3333	LYR552	3403	LYR622
3124	KXW233	3194	KYY923	3264	LLU623	3334	LYR553	3404	LYR623
3125	KXW234	3195	KYY924	3265	LLU624	3335	LYR554	3405	LYR624
3126	KXW235	3196	KYY925	3266	LLU625	3336	LYR555	3406	LYR625
3127	KXW236	3197	KYY926	3267	LLU626	3337	LYR556	3407	LYR626
3128	KXW237	3198	KYY927	3268	LLU627	3338	LYR557	3408	LYR627
3129	KXW238	3199	KYY928	3269	LLU628	3339	LYR558	3409	LYR628
3130	KXW239	3200	KYY929	3270	LLU629	3340	LYR559	3410	LYR629
3131	KXW240	3201	KYY930	3271	LLU630	3341	LYR560	3411	LYR630
3132	KXW241	3202	KYY931	3272	LLU631	3342	LYR561	3412	LYR631
3133	KXW242	3203	KYY932	3273	LLU632	3343	LYR562	3413	LYR632
3134	KXW243	3204	KYY933	3274	LLU633	3344	LYR563	3414	LYR633
3135	KXW244	3205	KYY934	3275	LLU634	3345	LYR564	3415	LYR634
3136	KXW245	3206	KYY935	3276	LLU635	3346	LYR565	3416	LYR635
3137	KXW246	3207	KYY936	3277	LLU636	3347	LYR566	3417	LYR836
3138	KXW247	3208	KYY937	3278	LLU637	3348	LYR567	3418	LYR837
3139	KXW248	3209	KYY938	3279	LLU638	3349	LYR568	3419	LYR838
3140	KXW249	3210	KYY939	3280	LLU639	3350	LYR569	3420	LYR839
3141	KXW250	3211	KYY940	3281	LLU640	3351	LYR570	3421	LYR840
3142	KYY871	3212	KYY941	3282	LYR501	3352	LYR571	3422	LYR841
3143	KYY872	3213	KYY942	3283	LYR502	3353	LYR572	3423	LYR842
3144	KYY873	3214	KYY943	3284	LYR503	3354	LYR573	3424	LYR843
3145	KYY874	3215	KYY944	3285	LYR504	3355	LYR574	3425	LYR844
3146	KYY875	3216	KYY945	3286	LYR505	3356	LYR575	3426	LYR845
3147	KYY876	3217	KYY946	3287	LYR506	3357	LYR576	3427	LYR846
3148	KYY877	3218	KYY947	3288	LYR507	3358	LYR577	3428	LYR847
3149	KYY878	3219	KYY948	3289	LYR508	3359	LYR578	3429	LYR848
3150	KYY879	3220	KYY949	3290	LYR509	3360	LYR579	3430	LYR849
3151	KYY880	3221	KYY950	3291	LYR510	3361	LYR580	3431	LYR850
3152	KYY881	3222	KYY951	3292	LYR511	3362	LYR581	3432	LYR851
3153	KYY882	3223	KYY952	3293	LYR512	3363	LYR582	3433	LYR852
3154	KYY883	3224	KYY953	3294	LYR513	3364	LYR583	3434	LYR853
3155	KYY884	3225	KYY954	3295	LYR514	3365	LYR584	3435	LYR854
3156	KYY885	3226	KYY955	3296	LYR515	3366	LYR585	3436	LYR855
3157	KYY886	3227	KYY956	3297	LYR516	3367	LYR586	3437	LYR856
3158	KYY887	3228	KYY957	3298	LYR517	3368	LYR587	3438	LYR857
3159	KYY888	3229	KYY958	3299	LYR518	3369	LYR588	3439	LYR858
3160	KYY889	3230	KYY959	3300	LYR519	3370	LYR589	3440	LYR859
3161	KYY890	3231	KYY960	3301	LYR520	3371	LYR590	3441	LYR860
3162	KYY891	3232	KYY961	3302	LYR521	3372	LYR591	3442	LYR861
3163	KYY892	3233	KYY962	3303	LYR522	3373	LYR592	3443	LYR862
3164	KYY893	3234	KYY963	3304	LYR523	3374	LYR593	3444	LYR863
3165	KYY894	3235	KYY964	3305	LYR524	3375	LYR594	3445	LYR864
3166	KYY895	3236	KYY965	3306	LYR525	3376	LYR595	3446	LYR865
3167	KYY896	3237	KYY966	3307	LYR526	3377	LYR596	3447	LYR866
3168	KYY897	3238	KYY967	3308	LYR527	3378	LYR597	3448	LYR867
3169	KYY898	3239	KYY968	3309	LYR528	3379	LYR598	3449	LYR868
3170	KYY899	3240	KYY969	3310	LYR529	3380	LYR599	3450	LYR869
3171	KYY900	3241	KYY970	3311	LYR530	3381	LYR600	3451	LYR870
3172	KYY901	3242	LLU601	3312	LYR531	3382	LYR601	3452	LYR871
3173	KYY902	3243	LLU602	3313	LYR532	3383	LYR602	3453	LYR872
3174	KYY903	3244	LLU603	3314	LYR533	3384	LYR603	3454	LYR873
3175	KYY904	3245	LLU604	3315	LYR534	3385	LYR604	3455	LYR874
3176	KYY905	3246	LLU605	3316	LYR535	3386	LYR605	3456	LYR875
3177	KYY906	3247	LLU606	3317	LYR536	3387	LYR606	3457	LYR876

RT		RT		RT		RT		RT	
3458	LYR877	3528	MLL838	3598	MLL908	3668	MXX183	3738	NLE845
3459	LYR878	3529	MLL839	3599	MLL909	3669	MXX184	3739	NLE846
3460	LYR879	3530	MLL840	3600	MLL910	3670	MXX185	3740	NLE847
3461	LYR880	3531	MLL841	3601	MLL911	3671	MXX186	3741	NLE848
3462	LYR881	3532	MLL842	3602	MLL912	3672	MXX187	3742	NLE849
3463	LYR882	3533	MLL843	3603	MLL913	3673	MXX188	3743	NLE850
3464	LYR883	3534	MLL844	3604	MLL914	3674	MXX189	3744	NLE851
3465	LYR884	3535	MLL845	3605	MLL915	3675	MXX190	3745	NLE852
3466	LYR885	3536	MLL846	3606	MLL916	3676	MXX191	3746	NLE853
3467	LYR886	3537	MLL847	3607	MLL917	3677	MXX192	3747	NLE854
3468	LYR887	3538	MLL848	3608	MLL918	3678	MXX193	3748	NLE855
3469	LYR888	3539	MLL849	3609	MLL919	3679	MXX194	3749	NLE856
3470	LYR889	3540	MLL850	3610	MLL920	3680	MXX195	3750	NLE857
3471	LYR890	3541	MLL851	3611	MLL921	3681	MXX196	3751	NLE858
3472	LYR891	3542	MLL852	3612	MLL922	3682	MXX197	3752	NLE859
3473	LYR892	3543	MLL853	3613	MLL923	3683	MXX198	3753	NLE860
3474	LYR893	3544	MLL854	3614	MLL924	3684	MXX199	3754	NLE861
3475	LYR894	3545	MLL855	3615	MLL925	3685	MXX200	3755	NLE862
3476	LYR895	3546	MLL856	3616	MXX131	3686	MXX201	3756	NLE863
3477	LYR896	3547	MLL857	3617	MXX132	3687	MXX202	3757	NLE864
3478	LYR897	3548	MLL858	3618	MXX133	3688	MXX203	3758	NLE865
3479	LYR898	3549	MLL859	3619	MXX134	3689	MXX204	3759	NLE866
3480	LYR899	3550	MLL860	3620	MXX135	3690	MXX205	3760	NLE867
3481	LYR900	3551	MLL861	3621	MXX136	3691	MXX206	3761	NLE868
3482	LYR901	3552	MLL862	3622	MXX137	3692	MXX207	3762	NLE869
3483	LYR902	3553	MLL863	3623	MXX138	3693	MXX208	3763	NLE870
3484	LYR903	3554	MLL864	3624	MXX139	3694	NLE801	3764	NLE871
3485	LYR904	3555	MLL865	3625	MXX140	3695	NLE802	3765	NLE872
3486	LYR905	3556	MLL866	3626	MXX141	3696	NLE803	3766	NLE873
3487	LYR906	3557	MLL867	3627	MXX142	3697	NLE804	3767	NLE874
3488	LYR907	3558	MLL868	3628	MXX143	3698	NLE805	3768	NLE875
3489	LYR908	3559	MLL869	3629	MXX144	3699	NLE806	3769	NLE876
3490	LYR909	3560	MLL870	3630	MXX145	3700	NLE807	3770	NLE877
3491	LYR910	3561	MLL871	3631	MXX146	3701	NLE808	3771	NLE878
3492	LYR911	3562	MLL872	3632	MXX147	3702	NLE809	3772	NLE879
3493	LYR912	3563	MLL873	3633	MXX148	3703	NLE810	3773	NLE880
3494	LYR913	3564	MLL874	3634	MXX149	3704	NLE811	3774	NLE881
3495	LYR914	3565	MLL875	3635	MXX150	3705	NLE812	3775	NLE882
3496	LYR915	3566	MLL876	3636	MXX151	3706	NLE813	3776	NLE883
3497	LYR916	3567	MLL877	3637	MXX152	3707	NLE814	3777	NLE884
3498	LYR917	3568	MLL878	3638	MXX153	3708	NLE815	3778	NLE885
3499	LYR918	3569	MLL879	3639	MXX154	3709	NLE816	3779	NLE886
3500	LYR919	3570	MLL880	3640	MXX155	3710	NLE817	3780	NLE887
3501	LYR920	3571	MLL881	3641	MXX156	3711	NLE818	3781	NLE888
3502	LYR921	3572	MLL882	3642	MXX157	3712	NLE819	3782	NLE889
3503	LYR922	3573	MLL883	3643	MXX158	3713	NLE820	3783	NLE890
3504	LYR923	3574	MLL884	3644	MXX159	3714	NLE821	3784	NLE891
3505	LYR924	3575	MLL885	3645	MXX160	3715	NLE822	3785	NLE892
3506	LYR925	3576	MLL886	3646	MXX161	3716	NLE823	3786	NLE893
3507	LYR926	3577	MLL887	3647	MXX162	3717	NLE824	3787	NLE894
3508	LYR927	3578	MLL888	3648	MXX163	3718	NLE825	3788	NLE895
3509	LYR928	3579	MLL889	3649	MXX164	3719	NLE826	3789	NLE896
3510	LYR929	3580	MLL890	3650	MXX165	3720	NLE827	3790	NLE897
3511	LYR930	3581	MLL891	3651	MXX166	3721	NLE828	3791	NLE898
3512	LYR931	3582	MLL892	3652	MXX167	3722	NLE829	3792	NLE899
3513	LYR932	3583	MLL893	3653	MXX168	3723	NLE830	3793	NLE900
3514	LYR933	3584	MLL894	3654	MXX169	3724	NLE831	3794	NXP801
3515	LYR934	3585	MLL895	3655	MXX170	3725	NLE832	3795	NXP802
3516	MLL826	3586	MLL896	3656	MXX171	3726	NLE833	3796	NXP803
3517	MLL827	3587	MLL897	3657	MXX172	3727	NLE834	3797	NXP804
3518	MLL828	3588	MLL898	3658	MXX173	3728	NLE835	3798	NXP805
3519	MLL829	3589	MLL899	3659	MXX174	3729	NLE836	3799	NXP806
3520	MLL830	3590	MLL900	3660	MXX175	3730	NLE837	3800	NXP807
3521	MLL831	3591	MLL901	3661	MXX176	3731	NLE838	3801	NXP808
3522	MLL832	3592	MLL902	3662	MXX177	3732	NLE839	3802	NXP809
3523	MLL833	3593	MLL903	3663	MXX178	3733	NLE840	3803	NXP810
3524	MLL834	3594	MLL904	3664	MXX179	3734	NLE841	3804	NXP811
3525	MLL835	3595	MLL905	3665	MXX180	3735	NLE842	3805	NXP812
3526	MLL836	3596	MLL906	3666	MXX181	3736	NLE843	3806	NXP813
3527	MLL837	3597	MLL907	3667	MXX182	3737	NLE844	3807	NXP814

RT		RT		RT		RT		RT	
3808	NXP815	3878	LLU677	3948	LUC107	4018	LUC177	4088	LUC437
3809	NXP816	3879	LLU678	3949	LUC108	4019	LUC178	4089	LUC438
3810	NXP817	3880	LLU679	3950	LUC109	4020	LUC179	4090	LUC439
3811	NXP818	3881	LLU680	3951	LUC110	4021	LUC180	4091	LUC440
3812	NXP819	3882	LLU681	3952	LUC111	4022	LUC181	4092	LUC441
3813	NXP820	3883	LLU682	3953	LUC112	4023	LUC182	4093	LUC442
3814	NXP821	3884	LLU683	3954	LUC113	4024	LUC183	4094	LUC443
3815	NXP822	3885	LLU684	3955	LUC114	4025	LUC184	4095	LUC444
3816	NXP823	3886	LLU685	3956	LUC115	4026	LUC185	4096	LUC445
3817	NXP824	3887	LLU686	3957	LUC116	4027	LUC186	4097	LUC446
3818	NXP825	3888	LLU687	3958	LUC117	4028	LUC187	4098	LUC447
3819	NXP826	3889	LLU688	3959	LUC118	4029	LUC188	4099	LUC448
3820	NXP827	3890	LLU689	3960	LUC119	4030	LUC189	4100	LUC449
3821	NXP828	3891	LLU690	3961	LUC120	4031	LUC190	4101	LUC450
3822	NXP829	3892	LLU691	3962	LUC121	4032	LUC191	4102	LUC451
3823	NXP830	3893	LLU692	3963	LUC122	4033	LUC192	4103	LUC452
3824	NXP831	3894	LLU693	3964	LUC123	4034	LUC193	4104	LUC453
3825	NXP832	3895	LLU694	3965	LUC124	4035	LUC194	4105	LUC454
3826	NXP833	3896	LLU695	3966	LUC125	4036	LUC195	4106	LUC455
3827	NXP834	3897	LLU696	3967	LUC126	4037	LUC196	4107	LUC456
3828	NXP835	3898	LLU697	3968	LUC127	4038	LUC197	4108	LUC457
3829	NXP836	3899	LLU698	3969	LUC128	4039	LUC198	4109	LUC458
3830	NXP837	3900	LLU699	3970	LUC129	4040	LUC199	4110	LUC459
3831	NXP838	3901	LLU700	3971	LUC130	4041	LUC200	4111	LUC460
3832	NXP839	3902	LLU701	3972	LUC131	4042	LUC391	4112	LUC461
3833	NXP840	3903	LLU702	3973	LUC132	4043	LUC392	4113	LUC462
3834	NXP841	3904	LLU703	3974	LUC133	4044	LUC393	4114	LUC463
3835	NXP842	3905	LLU704	3975	LUC134	4045	LUC394	4115	LUC464
3836	NXP843	3906	LLU705	3976	LUC135	4046	LUC395	4116	LUC465
3837	NXP844	3907	LLU706	3977	LUC136	4047	LUC396	4117	LUC466
3838	NXP845	3908	LLU707	3978	LUC137	4048	LUC397	4118	LUC467
3839	NXP846	3909	LLU708	3979	LUC138	4049	LUC398	4119	LUC468
3840	NXP847	3910	LLU709	3980	LUC139	4050	LUC399	4120	LUC469
3841	NXP848	3911	LLU710	3981	LUC140	4051	LUC400	4121	LUC470
3842	LLU641	3912	LLU711	3982	LUC141	4052	LUC401	4122	LUC471
3843	LLU642	3913	LLU712	3983	LUC142	4053	LUC402	4123	LUC472
3844	LLU643	3914	LLU713	3984	LUC143	4054	LUC403	4124	LUC473
3845	LLU644	3915	LLU714	3985	LUC144	4055	LUC404	4125	LUC474
3846	LLU645	3916	LLU715	3986	LUC145	4056	LUC405	4126	LUC475
3847	LLU646	3917	LLU716	3987	LUC146	4057	LUC406	4127	LUC476
3848	LLU647	3918	LLU717	3988	LUC147	4058	LUC407	4128	LUC477
3849	LLU648	3919	LLU718	3989	LUC148	4059	LUC408	4129	LUC478
3850	LLU649	3920	LLU719	3990	LUC149	4060	LUC409	4130	LUC479
3851	LLU650	3921	LLU720	3991	LUC150	4061	LUC410	4131	LUC480
3852	LLU651	3922	LLU721	3992	LUC151	4062	LUC411	4132	LUC481
3853	LLU652	3923	LLU722	3993	LUC152	4063	LUC412	4133	LUC482
3854	LLU653	3924	LLU723	3994	LUC153	4064	LUC413	4134	LUC483
3855	LLU654	3925	LLU724	3995	LUC154	4065	LUC414	4135	LUC484
3856	LLU655	3926	LLU725	3996	LUC155	4066	LUC415	4136	LUC485
3857	LLU656	3927	LLU726	3997	LUC156	4067	LUC416	4137	LUC486
3858	LLU657	3928	LLU727	3998	LUC157	4068	LUC417	4138	LUC487
3859	LLU658	3929	LLU728	3999	LUC158	4069	LUC418	4139	LUC488
3860	LLU659	3930	LLU729	4000	LUC159	4070	LUC419	4140	LUC489
3861	LLU660	3931	LLU730	4001	LUC160	4071	LUC420	4141	LUC490
3862	LLU661	3992	LLU731	4002	LUC161	4072	LUC421	4142	LYF201
3863	LLU662	3933	LLU732	4003	LUC162	4073	LUC422	4143	LYF202
3864	LLU663	3934	LLU733	4004	LUC163	4074	LUC423	4144	LYF203
3865	LLU664	3935	LLU734	4005	LUC164	4075	LUC424	4145	LYF204
3866	LLU665	3936	LLU735	4006	LUC165	4076	LUC425	4146	LYF205
3867	LLU666	3937	LLU736	4007	LUC166	4077	LUC426	4147	LYF206
3868	LLU667	3938	LLU737	4008	LUC167	4078	LUC427	4148	LYF207
3869	LLU668	3939	LLU738	4009	LUC168	4079	LUC428	4149	LYF208
3870	LLU669	3940	LLU739	4010	LUC169	4080	LUC429	4150	LYF209
3871	LLU670	3941	LLU740	4011	LUC170	4081	LUC430	4151	LYF210
3872	LLU671	3942	LUC101	4012	LUC171	4082	LUC431	4152	LYF211
3873	LLU672	3943	LUC102	4013	LUC172	4083	LUC432	4153	LYF212
3874	LLU673	3944	LUC103	4014	LUC173	4084	LUC433	4154	LYF213
3875	LLU674	3945	LUC104	4015	LUC174	4085	LUC434	4155	LYF214
3876	LLU675	3946	LUC105	4016	LUC175	4086	LUC435	4156	LYF215
3877	LLU676	3947	LUC106	4017	LUC176	4087	LUC436	4157	LYF216

RT		RT		RT		RT		RT	
4158	LYF217	4228	KYY831	4298	NLE962	4368	NLP533	4438	NXP792
4159	LYF218	4229	KYY832	4299	NLE963	4369	NLP534	4439	NXP793
4160	LYF219	4230	KYY833	4300	NLE964	4370	NLP535	4440	NXP794
4161	LYF220	4231	KYY834	4301	NLE965	4371	NLP536	4441	NXP795
4162	LYF221	4232	KYY835	4302	NLE966	4372	NLP537	4442	NXP796
4163	LYF222	4233	KYY836	4303	NLE967	4373	NLP538	4443	NXP797
4164	LYF223	4234	KYY837	4304	NLE968	4374	NLP539	4444	NXP798
4165	LYF224	4235	KYY838	4305	NLE969	4375	NLP540	4445	NXP799
4166	LYF225	4236	KYY839	4306	NLE970	4376	NLP541	4446	NXP800
4167	LYF226	4237	KYY840	4307	NLE971	4377	NLP542	4447	OLD667
4168	LYF227	4238	KYY841	4308	NLE972	4378	NLP543	4448	OLD668
4169	LYF228	4239	KYY842	4309	NLE973	4379	NLP544	4449	OLD679
4170	LYF229	4240	KYY843	4310	NLE974	4380	NLP545	4450	OLD680
4171	LYF230	4241	KYY844	4311	NLE975	4381	NLP546	4451	OLD671
4172	LYF231	4242	KYY845	4312	NLE976	4382	NLP547	4452	OLD672
4173	LYF232	4243	KYY846	4313	NLE977	4383	NLP548	4453	OLD673
4174	LYF233	4244	KYY847	4314	NLE978	4384	NLP549	4454	OLD674
4175	LYF234	4245	KYY848	4315	NLE979	4385	NLP550	4455	OLD675
4176	LYF235	4246	KYY849	4316	NLE980	4386	NLP551	4456	OLD676
4177	LYF236	4247	KYY850	4317	NLE981	4387	NLP552	4457	OLD677
4178	LYF237	4248	KYY851	4318	NLE982	4388	NLP553	4458	OLD678
4179	LYF238	4249	KYY852	4319	NLE983	4389	NLP554	4459	OLD679
4180	LYF239	4250	KYY853	4320	NLE984	4390	NLP555	4460	OLD680
4181	LYF240	4251	KYY854	4321	NLE985	4391	NLP556	4461	OLD681
4182	LYF241	4252	KYY855	4322	NLE986	4392	NLP557	4462	OLD682
4183	LYF242	4253	KYY856	4323	NLE987	4393	NLP558	4463	OLD683
4184	LYF243	4254	KYY857	4324	NLE988	4394	NLP559	4464	OLD684
4185	LYF244	4255	KYY858	4325	NLE989	4395	NLP560	4465	OLD685
4186	LYF245	4256	KYY859	4326	NLE990	4396	NLP561	4466	OLD686
4187	LYF246	4257	KYY860	4327	NLE991	4397	NXP751	4467	OLD687
4188	LYF247	4258	KYY861	4328	NLE992	4398	NXP752	4468	OLD688
4189	LYF248	4259	KYY862	4329	NLE993	4399	NXP753	4469	OLD689
4190	LYF249	4260	KYY863	4330	NLE994	4400	NXP754	4470	OLD690
4191	LYF250	4261	KYY864	4331	NLE995	4401	NXP755	4471	OLD691
4192	LYF251	4262	KYY865	4332	NLE996	4402	NXP756	4472	OLD692
4193	LYF252	4263	KYY866	4333	NLE997	4403	NXP757	4473	OLD693
4194	LYF253	4264	KYY867	4334	NLE998	4404	NXP758	4474	OLD694
4195	LYF254	4265	KYY868	4335	NLE999	4405	NXP759	4475	OLD695
4196	LYF255	4266	KYY869	4336	NLP501	4406	NXP760	4476	OLD696
4197	LYF256	4267	KYY870	4337	NLP502	4407	NXP761	4477	OLD697
4198	LYF257	4268	NLE932	4338	NLP503	4408	NXP762	4478	OLD698
4199	LYF258	4269	NLE933	4339	NLP504	4409	NXP763	4479	OLD699
4200	LYF259	4270	NLE934	4340	NLP505	4410	NXP764	4480	OLD700
4201	LYF260	4271	NLE935	4341	NLP506	4411	NXP765	4481	OLD701
4202	LYF261	4272	NLE936	4342	NLP507	4412	NXP766	4482	OLD702
4203	LYF262	4273	NLE937	4343	NLP508	4413	NXP767	4483	OLD703
4204	LYF263	4274	NLE938	4344	NLP509	4414	NXP768	4484	OLD704
4205	LYF264	4275	NLE939	4345	NLP510	4415	NXP769	4485	OLD705
4206	LYF265	4276	NLE940	4346	NLP511	4416	NXP770	4486	OLD706
4207	LYF266	4277	NLE941	4347	NLP512	4417	NXP771	4487	OLD707
4208	LYF267	4278	NLE942	4348	NLP513	4418	NXP772	4488	OLD708
4209	LYF268	4279	NLE943	4349	NLP514	4419	NXP773	4489	OLD709
4210	LYF269	4280	NLE944	4350	NLP515	4420	NXP774	4490	OLD710
4211	LYF270	4281	NLE945	4351	NLP516	4421	NXP775	4491	OLD711
4212	LYF271	4282	NLE946	4352	NLP517	4422	NXP776	4492	OLD712
4213	LYF272	4283	NLE947	4353	NLP518	4423	NXP777	4493	OLD713
4214	LYF273	4284	NLE948	4354	NLP519	4424	NXP778	4494	OLD714
4215	LYF274	4285	NLE949	4355	NLP520	4425	NXP779	4495	OLD715
4216	LYF275	4286	NLE950	4356	NLP521	4426	NXP780	4496	OLD716
4217	LYF276	4287	NLE951	4357	NLP522	4427	NXP781	4497	OLD717
4218	KYY821	4288	NLE952	4358	NLP523	4428	NXP782	4498	OLD718
4219	KYY822	4289	NLE953	4359	NLP524	4429	NXP783	4499	OLD719
4220	KYY823	4290	NLE954	4360	NLP525	4430	NXP784	4500	OLD720
4221	KYY824	4291	NLE955	4361	NLP526	4431	NXP785	4501	OLD721
4222	KYY825	4292	NLE956	4362	NLP527	4432	NXP786	4502	OLD722
4223	KYY826	4293	NLE957	4363	NLP528	4433	NXP787	4503	OLD723
4224	KYY827	4294	NLE958	4364	NLP529	4434	NXP788	4504	OLD724
4225	KYY828	4295	NLE959	4365	NLP530	4435	NXP789	4505	OLD725
4226	KYY829	4296	NLE960	4366	NLP531	4436	NXP790	4506	OLD726
4227	KYY830	4297	NLE961	4367	NLP532	4437	NXP791	4507	OLD727

RT

RT		RT		RT		RT		RT	
4508	OLD728	4572	NLP565	4636	NXP889	4700	NXP985	4764	OLD551
4509	OLD729	4573	NLP566	4637	NXP890	4701	NXP986	4765	OLD552
4510	OLD730	4574	NLP567	4638	NXP891	4702	NXP987	4766	OLD553
4511	OLD731	4575	NLP568	4639	NXP892	4703	NXP988	4767	OLD554
4512	OLD732	4576	NLP569	4640	NXP893	4704	NXP989	4768	OLD555
4513	OLD733	4577	NLP570	4641	NXP894	4705	NXP990	4769	OLD556
4514	OLD734	4578	NLP571	4642	NXP895	4706	NXP991	4770	OLD557
4515	OLD735	4579	NLP572	4643	NXP896	4707	NXP992	4771	OLD558
4516	OLD736	4580	NLP573	4644	NXP897	4708	NXP993	4772	OLD559
4517	OLD737	4581	NLP574	4645	NXP898	4709	NXP994	4773	OLD560
4518	OLD738	4582	NLP575	4646	NXP899	4710	NXP995	4774	OLD561
4519	OLD739	4583	NLP576	4647	NXP900	4711	NXP996	4775	OLD562
4520	OLD740	4584	NLP577	4648	NXP901	4712	NXP997	4776	OLD563
4521	OLD741	4585	NLP578	4649	NXP902	4713	NXP998	4777	OLD564
4522	OLD742	4586	NLP579	4650	NXP903	4714	NXP999	4778	OLD565
4523	OLD743	4587	NLP580	4651	NXP904	4715	OLD501	4779	OLD566
4524	OLD744	4588	NLP581	4652	NXP905	4716	OLD502	4780	OLD567
4525	OLD745	4589	NLP582	4653	NXP906	4717	OLD503	4781	OLD568
4526	OLD746	4590	NLP583	4654	NXP907	4718	OLD504	4782	OLD569
4527	OLD747	4591	NLP584	4655	NXP908	4719	OLD505	4783	OLD570
4528	OLD748	4592	NLP585	4656	NXP909	4720	OLD506	4784	OLD821
4529	OLD749	4593	NLP586	4657	NXP910	4721	OLD507	4785	OLD822
4530	OLD750	4594	NLP587	4658	NXP911	4722	OLD508	4786	OLD823
4531	OLD751	4595	NLP588	4659	NXP912	4723	OLD509	4787	OLD824
4532	OLD752	4596	NLP589	4660	NXP913	4724	OLD510	4788	OLD825
4533	OLD753	4597	NLP590	4661	NXP914	4725	OLD511	4789	OLD826
4534	OLD754	4598	NLP591	4662	NXP915	4726	OLD512	4790	OLD827
4535	OLD755	4599	NLP592	4663	NXP916	4727	OLD513	4791	OLD828
4536	OLD756	4600	NLP593	4664	NXP917	4728	OLD514	4792	OLD829
4537	OLD757	4601	NLP594	4665	NXP918	4729	OLD515	4793	OLD830
4538	OLD758	4602	NLP595	4666	NXP919	4730	OLD516	4794	OLD861
4539	OLD759	4603	NLP596	4667	NXP920	4731	OLD517	4795	NXP937
4540	OLD760	4604	NLP597	4668	MXX40	4732	OLD518	4796	NXP938
4541	OLD761	4605	NLP598	4669	NXP921	4733	OLD519	4797	NXP939
4542	OLD762	4606	NLP599	4670	NXP922	4734	OLD520	4798	NXP940
4543	OLD763	4607	NLP600	4671	NXP923	4735	OLD521	4799	NXP941
4544	OLD764	4608	NXP861	4672	NXP924	4736	OLD522	4800	NXP942
4545	OLD765	4609	NXP862	4673	NXP925	4737	OLD523	4801	NXP943
4546	OLD766	4610	NXP863	4674	NXP926	4738	OLD524	4802	NXP944
4547	OLD767	4611	NXP864	4675	NXP927	4739	OLD525	4803	NXP945
4548	OLD768	4612	NXP865	4676	NXP928	4740	OLD526	4804	NXP946
4549	OLD769	4613	NXP866	4677	NXP929	4741	OLD527	4805	NXP947
4550	OLD770	4614	NXP867	4678	NXP930	4742	OLD528	4806	NXP948
4551	OLD771	4615	NXP868	4679	NXP931	4743	OLD529	4807	NXP949
4552	OLD772	4616	NXP869	4680	NXP932	4744	OLD530	4808	NXP950
4553	OLD773	4617	NXP870	4681	NXP933	4745	OLD531	4809	NXP951
4554	OLD774	4618	NXP871	4682	NXP934	4746	OLD532	4810	NXP952
4555	OLD775	4619	NXP872	4683	NXP935	4747	OLD533	4811	NXP953
4556	OLD776	4620	NXP873	4684	NXP936	4748	OLD534	4812	NXP954
4557	NXP849	4621	NXP874	4685	NXP970	4749	OLD535	4813	OLD577
4558	NXP850	4622	NXP875	4686	NXP971	4750	OLD537	4814	OLD578
4559	NXP851	4623	NXP876	4687	NXP972	4751	OLD538	4815	OLD579
4560	NXP852	4624	NXP877	4688	NXP973	4752	OLD539	4816	OLD580
4561	NXP853	4625	NXP878	4689	NXP974	4753	OLD540	4817	OLD581
4562	NXP854	4626	NXP879	4690	NXP975	4754	OLD541	4818	OLD582
4563	NXP855	4627	NXP880	4691	NXP976	4755	OLD542	4819	OLD583
4564	NXP856	4628	NXP881	4692	NXP977	4756	OLD543	4820	OLD584
4565	NXP857	4629	NXP882	4693	NXP978	4757	OLD544	4821	OLD585
4566	NXP858	4630	NXP883	4694	NXP979	4758	OLD545	4822	OLD586
4567	NXP859	4631	NXP884	4695	NXP980	4759	OLD546	4823	OLD587
4568	NXP860	4632	NXP885	4696	NXP981	4760	OLD547	4824	OLD588
4569	NLP562	4633	NXP886	4697	NXP982	4761	OLD548	4825	OLD589
4570	NLP563	4634	NXP887	4698	NXP983	4762	OLD549		
4571	NLP564	4635	NXP888	4699	NXP984	4763	OLD550		

s   RT 106 was transferred to the service vehicle fleet as 1036TV
RT 1420's chassis was transferred to the service vehicle fleet as 1037J

Prototype RTL 501 was the only Leyland fitted with a standard RT3 body, giving it the distinctive appearance evident in this view at Well Hall station. It was withdrawn in 1958 after ten years service. A.B. Cross

RTL

To meet the unprecedented requirements for new vehicles immediately after the Second World War, London Transport decided to purchase part of its new fleet from Leyland Motors Ltd. An initial order for 1,000 7ft 6in wide chassis was placed in 1947 and this was supplemented by further orders until a total of 1,631 was reached. The RTL chassis was based on the standard Titan PD2/1 model modified to make it as comparable as possible to the AEC RT. The chassis frame had the same outline as the RT and the specification included the AEC preselective gearbox and fluid flywheel, which were not offered on the standard Titan. The engine was the new Leyland 9.8 litre model which developed 125 bhp at 1,800 rpm, derated by LT to 115 bhp for fuel economy. The original intention had been that the first 1,000 chassis would be bodied by Metro-Cammell to the standard RT3 specification but this was later altered to a modified version of the company's standard product. This had a different method of body mounting and was not interchangeable with other RTs and RTLs. London Transport therefore reduced the order to 450 and in compensation placed the entire order for the RF class with MCW. Most of the remaining bodies were supplied by Park Royal but the last thirty had Weymann bodywork.

The prototype was numbered RTL 501, as the first five hundred numbers were originally reserved for the RTWs. It took the body and registration number intended for RT 657 and was therefore the only RTL built with an RT3 body. RTL 501 entered

Only thirty-two bodies were supplied by Weymann of Addlestone for Leyland chassis, an odd one on RTL 1307 for its American tour and a final batch of thirty-one in 1954. Most of the 1954 batch went straight into store and did not enter service until 1958, which is when newly licensed RTL 1609 was photographed at Victoria, running from Dalston garage on a Sunday only working on route 38. W. Legg

service at Turnham Green garage on 16th June 1948 and delivery of the production buses from Park Royal began on 24th November 1948. The first Metro-Cammell bus (RTL 551) was received on 11th August 1949 and Weymann RTL 1601 was taken into stock on 5th May 1954, but the rest of the Weymanns were delivered between August and November 1954. Apart from the Metro-Cammells, the bodywork modifications followed the same pattern as the RTs. Following a prototype modification to RTL 1337, from RTL 1469 onwards the front end of the chassis frame was strengthened and the steering geometry modified. These were later classified 2/7RTL. These modifications were never made on the remainder of the class. The last RTLs were delivered from Park Royal on 29th September and Weymann on 10th November 1954. Sixty-three were not required for service and were placed in store, mainly at Garston garage (RTLs 1568–1600 and 1602–1631). None of these was licensed until February and March 1958, when they were used to replace earlier vehicles which were then sold, withdrawal of the class having started in January 1958. An earlier withdrawal was RTL 1222, burnt out in January 1953. RTL 1581 was also lost through fire, in June 1958.

RTL 1307 was specially fitted with a Weymann body when new in 1952 so that both manufacturers could be represented on the tour of north America. It was fitted out as an information office. RTL 1459 went to Switzerland with RT 3710 in 1953, RTL 1117 visited Holland for Arnhem Week in May 1955 and RTL 1486 Helsinki with RT 2422 in June 1957.

In line with the rest of the fleet, the RTLs were fitted with flashing trafficators in 1959/1960 and received the same modified layout of rear arrows as the RTs in 1962.

The last thirty-three RTLs bodied by Park Royal also went straight into store in 1954 and were not licensed until 1958. Like all of the class from RTL 1469 onwards, RTL 1591, seen here at Bank, was a 2/7RT8/2. A.B. Cross

Although structurally quite different from the standard RT8 body, the 450 RT7 type bodies supplied by Metro-Cammell Carriage and Wagon Co. Ltd were externally an almost perfect copy, the only visible difference being the inverted gutter above the central cantrail band. RTL 975 was still working from its original garage, Camberwell, when photographed on the last day of route 48, 19th August 1958. A.B. Cross

Eighteen Leylands were painted green when overhauled in 1959 but were not welcome in the country area, did not go into service until July 1960 and were withdrawn again in June 1961. RTL 1311, seen parked at the new Hatfield garage, was the highest numbered of these and, like the rest, went straight into the training fleet when it left Hatfield, the first of the class to do so.
W.R. Legg

RTLs were not strangers to Country Buses as they were borrowed from Central Buses during summer weekends to run the heavily augmented Sunday services.
Metro-Cammell bodied RTL 825 was on loan at Staines when photographed on August Bank Holiday 1955.
A.B. Cross

RTL 1491, one of the final production run of 163 Leylands delivered in 1954 operates an unscheduled extra on route 103 in South Street Romford, one of the many which were put on to routes where the 1958 service cuts had been too severe. A.B. Cross

Two RTLs were fitted with RT10 bodies in 1956, RTLs 9 and 36, but both were sold in 1958 and no more had been done by the end of 1962. In this form they were very similar in appearance to prototype RTL 501, as is apparent in this photograph of RTL 9 at Shepherds Bush. W.R. Legg

The highly respected Scottish independent, A & C McLennan of Spitalfield, bought five of the RTLs which were sold off in 1958. The company's smart blue and cream paint scheme was well suited to RTL 40's Park Royal body of 1948, here on display in Kinnoul Street, Perth.
Ken Glazier

Chassis: Leyland Titan 7RT
Engine: Leyland O600 6-cylinder 9.8 litre oil 125 bhp (derated to 115bhp)
Transmission: AEC D140 4-speed air operated preselective with fluid flywheel
Bodywork: Park Royal (originally 1–550, 1001–1306, 1308–1600); Metro-Cammell (551–1000); Weymann (originally 1307, 1601–1631)
Capacity: H56R
L.T. chassis codes: 7RT (1–550, 1001–1336, 1338–1468); 1/7RT (551–1000): 2/7RT; 1337, 1469–1631:
Body codes: RT3 (501); RT3/1 (1–118); RT7 (551–1000); RT8 (119–500, 502–550, 1001–1312); RT8/2 (1313–1631); RT10 (9, 36 from October 1956)
Built: 1948–1954
Number built: 1631
Number in stock: 1.1.55: 1631   31.12.62: 1332

RTL		Date out of stock	RTL		Date out of stock	RTL		Date out of stock
1	JXN313	10.2.58	53	JXN376		105	JXN428	8.12.58
2	JXN314	11.3.58	54	JXN377	28.1.58	106	JXN429	14.1.59
3	JXN315		55	JXN378	10.2.58	107	JXN430	
4	JXN316	28.2.58	56	JXN379		108	JXN431	14.1.59
5	JXN317	28.2.58	57	JXN380	9.3.59	109	JXN432	14.1.59
6	JXN318	17.3.58	58	JXN381	14.1.59	110	JXN433	
7	JXN319	17.3.58	59	JXN382	8.12.58	111	JXN434	9.3.59
8	JXN320	28.8.58	60	JXN383		112	JXN435	
9	JXN321	17.3.58	61	JXN384	14.1.59	113	JXN436	9.3.59
10	JXN322	14.3.58	62	JXN385	14.1.59	114	JXN437	
11	JXN323	26.9.58	63	JXN386	8.12.58	115	JXN438	9.3.59
12	JXN324	26.9.58	64	JXN387		116	JXN439	8.12.58
13	JXN333	26.9.58	65	JXN388		117	KGK781	8.12.58
14	JXN334	25.1.58	66	JXN389		118	KGK782	8.12.58
15	JXN335	26.9.58	67	JXN390		119	KGK783	
16	JXN336	28.8.58	68	JXN391		120	KGK784	
17	JXN337	20.2.58	69	JXN392		121	KGK785	
18	JXN338	5.2.58	70	JXN393		122	KGK786	
19	JXN339		71	JXN394	8.12.58	123	KGK787	
20	JXN340	26.9.58	72	JXN395		124	KGK788	
21	JXN341	14.2.58	73	JXN396		125	KGK789	8.12.58
22	JXN342		74	JXN397		126	KGK790	8.12.58
23	JXN344	28.2.58	75	JXN398		127	KGK791	
24	JXN347	24.7.58	76	JXN399	14.1.59	128	KGK792	
25	JXN348	11.3.58	77	JXN400		129	KGK793	26.4.62
26	JXN349	4.7.58	78	JXN401	8.12.58	130	KGK794	
27	JXN350	12.6.58	79	JXN402	14.1.59	131	KGK795	8.12.58
28	JXN351	14.3.58	80	JXN403	9.3.59	132	KGK796	
29	JXN352	25.1.58	81	JXN404	8.12.58	133	KGK797	16.1.59
30	JXN353	25.1.58	82	JXN405	9.3.59	134	KGK798	
31	JXN354	10.2.58	83	JXN406	14.1.59	135	KGK799	16.1.59
32	JXN355		84	JXN407	8.12.58	136	KGK800	14.1.59
33	JXN356	1.3.58	85	JXN408		137	KGK801	
34	JXN357	4.7.58	86	JXN409		138	KGK802	24.12.58
35	JXN358	6.2.58	87	JXN410	9.3.59	139	KGK803	
36	JXN359	12.6.58	88	JXN411		140	KGK804	
37	JXN360	25.1.58	89	JXN412		141	KGK805	
38	JXN361	28.3.58	90	JXN413		142	KGK806	
39	JXN362	28.3.58	91	JXN414	14.1.59	143	KGK807	
40	JXN363	12.6.58	92	JXN415		144	KGK808	
41	JXN364	25.1.58	93	JXN416	9.3.59	145	KGK809	
42	JXN365	23.6.58	94	JXN417	8.12.58	146	KGK810	
43	JXN366	14.2.58	95	JXN418	14.1.59	147	KGK811	
44	JXN367	14.2.58	96	JXN419		148	KGK812	
45	JXN368	19.3.58	97	JXN420	9 3.59	149	KGK813	24.12.58
46	JXN369	23.6.58	98	JXN421		150	KGK814	
47	JXN370	19.3.58	99	JXN422	14.1.59	151	KGK815	
48	JXN371	1.3.58	100	JXN423	8.12.58	152	KGK816	
49	JXN372	6.2.58	101	JXN424		153	KGK817	9.3.59
50	JXN373		102	JXN425	14.1.59	154	KGK818	
51	JXN374	20.2.58	103	JXN426	14.1.59	155	KGK819	8.12.58
52	JXN375	14.2.58	104	JXN427	9.3.59	156	KGK820	

RTL		Date out of stock	RTL		Date out of stock	RTL		Date out of stock
157	KGK821		227	KGK891	14.1.59	297	KGU255	9.3.59
158	KGK822	8.12.58	228	KGK892	14.1.59	298	KGU256	9.3.59
159	KGK823	9.3.59	229	KGK893		299	KGU257	
160	KGK824	14.1.59	230	KGK894	8.12.58	300	KGU258	13.1.61
161	KGK825		231	KGK895	14.1.59	301	KGU259	
162	KGK826	8.12.58	232	KGK896	8.12.58	302	KGU260	14.1.59
163	KGK827		233	KGK897	14.1.59	303	KGU261	9.3.59
164	KGK828		234	KGK898	8.12.58	304	KGU262	
165	KGK829		235	KGK899	14.1.59	305	KGU263	24.8.59
166	KGK830		236	KGK900	8.12.58	306	KGU264	9.3.59
167	KGK831	14.1.59	237	KGK901		307	KGU265	9.3.59
168	KGK832	5.12.58	238	KGK902		308	KGU266	
169	KGK833		239	KGK903	8.12.58	309	KGU267	9.3.59
170	KGK834		240	KGK904	9.3.59	310	KGU268	
171	KGK835	8.12.58	241	KGK905		311	KGU269	9.3.59
172	KGK836		242	KGK906	8.12.58	312	KGU270	
173	KGK837		243	KGK907	9.3.59	313	KGU271	
174	KGK838	17.5.60	244	KGK908		314	KGU272	
175	KGK839		245	KGK909	8.12.58	315	KGU273	
176	KGK840		246	KGK910		316	KGU274	
177	KGK841		247	KGK911		317	KGU275	
178	KGK842		248	KGK912		318	KGU276	9.3.59
179	KGK843		249	KGK913	14.1.59	319	KGU277	
180	KGK844		250	KGK914	9.3.59	320	KGU278	13.1.61
181	KGK845		251	KGK915	14.1.59	321	KGU279	
182	KGK846		252	KGK916	8.12.58	322	KGU280	
183	KGK847		253	KGK929	14.1.59	323	KGU281	9.3.59
184	KGK848		254	KGK930	8.12.58	324	KGU282	
185	KGK849	8.12.58	255	KGU201	14.1.59	325	KGU283	
186	KGK850	8.12.58	256	KGU202		326	KGU284	
187	KGK851	8.12.58	257	KGU203	8.12.58	327	KGU285	
188	KGK852	8.12.58	258	KGU204	14.1.59	328	KGU286	9.3.59
189	KGK853	8.12.58	259	KGU205	8.12.58	329	KGU287	
190	KGK854		260	KGU206		330	KGU288	
191	KGK855	8.12.58	261	KGU207	14.1.59	331	KGU289	
192	KGK856	9.3.59	262	KGU208	14.1.59	332	KGU401	9.3.59
193	KGK857	8.12.58	263	KGU209	8.12.58	333	KGU402	
194	KGK858	14.1.59	264	KGU210	8.12.58	334	KGU403	
195	KGK859	8.12.58	265	KGU211	9.3.59	335	KGU404	
196	KGK860	8.12.58	266	KGU212		336	KGU405	7.10.59
197	KGK861	8.12.58	267	KGU213	14.1.59	337	KGU406	
198	KGK862		268	KGU214	9.3.59	338	KGU407	
199	KGK863		269	KGU215	21.7.59	339	KGU408	
200	KGK864		270	KGU216	7.10.59	340	KGU409	
201	KGK865		271	KGU217	9.3.59	341	KGU417	
202	KGK866	14.1.59	272	KGU218	14.1.59	342	KGU418	
203	KGK867	8.12.58	273	KGU219	8.12.58	343	KGU419	
204	KGK868	8.12.58	274	KGU220	9.3.59	344	KGU420	
205	KGK869		275	KGU221	8.12.58	345	KGU421	
206	KGK870	8.12.58	276	KGU222	18.8.59	346	KGU422	
207	KGK871	8.12.58	277	KGU223		347	KGU423	
208	KGK872		278	KGU224	24.8.59	348	KGU424	
209	KGK873	14.1.59	279	KGU225	9.3.59	349	KGU425	13.1.61
210	KGK874	8.12.58	280	KGU226	8.12.58	350	KGU426	
211	KGK875	8.12.58	281	KGU227	14.1.59	351	KGU427	
212	KGK876	9.3.59	282	KGU228	8.12.58	352	KGU428	
213	KGK877	8.12.58	283	KGU229	14.1.59	353	KGU429	
214	KGK878	14.1.59	284	KGU230	9.3.59	354	KGU430	
215	KGK879	9.3.59	285	KGU231		355	KGU431	13.1.61
216	KGK880	8.12.58	286	KGU244	9.3.59	356	KGU432	13.1.61
217	KGK881	8.12.58	287	KGU245	8.12.58	357	KGU433	7.10.59
218	KGK882	8.12.58	288	KGU246	8.12.58	358	KGU434	21.7.59
219	KGK883	9.3.59	289	KGU247		359	KGU435	
220	KGK884	8.12.58	290	KGU248	9.3.59	360	KGU436	
221	KGK885	8.12.58	291	KGU249	9.3.59	361	KGU437	13.1.61
222	KGK886		292	KGU250	9.3.59	362	KGU438	24.8.59
223	KGK887		293	KGU251		363	KGU439	
224	KGK888	14.1.59	294	KGU252		364	KGU451	13.1.61
225	KGK889	9.3.59	295	KGU253		365	KGU452	
226	KGK890	8.12.58	296	KGU254		366	KGU453	

RTL		Date out of stock	RTL		Date out of stock	RTL		Date out of stock
367	KGU454		437	KLB624		507	KXW290	
368	KGU455		438	KLB625		508	KXW291	
369	KGU456		439	KLB626		509	KXW292	
370	KGU457		440	KLB627		510	KXW293	
371	KGU458		441	KLB628		511	KXW294	27.2.58
372	KGU459		442	KLB629		512	KXW295	
373	KGU460		443	KLB630		513	KXW296	27.2.58
374	KGU461		444	KLB639		514	KXW297	
375	KGU462		445	KLB640		515	KXW298	22.4.58
376	KGU463		446	KLB641	13.1.61	516	KXW299	27.2.58
377	KGU464		447	KLB642		517	KXW300	
378	KGU465		448	KLB643		518	KXW344	
379	KGU466		449	KLB644	13.1.61	519	KXW345	27.2.58
380	KGU467		450	KLB645		520	KXW346	27.2.58
381	KGU468		451	KLB646		521	KXW347	
382	KGU469		452	KLB647		522	KXW348	
383	KGU470		453	KLB648		523	KXW349	6.3.59
384	KGU471		454	KLB649		524	KXW350	
385	KGU472		455	KLB650		525	KYY521	6.3.59
386	KGU473		456	KLB651		526	KYY522	
387	KGU474		457	KLB652		527	KYY523	
388	KGU475		458	KLB653		528	KYY524	
389	KGU476		459	KLB654		529	KYY558	
390	KGU477		460	KLB679	6.3.59	530	KYY559	22.4.58
391	KGU478		461	KLB680		531	KYY560	
392	KGU479		462	KLB681		532	KYY561	
393	KGU480	13.1.61	463	KLB682	27.2.58	533	KYY562	
394	KGU481		464	KLB683	9.3.59	534	KYY563	
395	KGU482		465	KLB684		535	KYY564	
396	KGU483		466	KLB685		536	KYY565	
397	KGU484	13.1.61	467	KLB686		537	KYY566	22.4.58
398	KGU485		468	KLB687		538	KYY567	
399	KGU486		469	KLB688		539	KYY568	
400	KGU487		470	KLB689		540	KYY633	
401	KGU488	21.7.59	471	KLB690		541	KYY634	13.1.61
402	KGU489		472	KLB691		542	KYY635	
403	KGU490		473	KLB692		543	KYY636	
404	KGU491	13.1.61	474	KLB693		544	KYY637	
405	KGU492		475	KLB694		545	KYY638	13.1.61
406	KGU493		476	KLB695		546	KYY639	
407	KGU494		477	KLB696	22.4.58	547	KYY640	
408	KGU495		478	KLB697		548	KYY641	
409	KGU496		479	KLB698		549	KYY642	
410	KGU497		480	KLB699		550	KYY643	24.8.59
411	KGU498	6.3.59	481	KLB700	22.4.58	551	KGU1	
412	KGU499		482	KLB701		552	KGU2	
413	KGU500	27.2.58	483	KLB702		553	KGU3	
414	KLB601		484	KLB703		554	KGU4	
415	KLB602		485	KLB704	6.3.59	555	KGU5	
416	KLB603		486	KLB705		556	KGU6	
417	KLB604		487	KLB706		557	KGU7	
418	KLB605		488	KLB707		558	KGU8	
419	KLB606		489	KLB708		559	KGU9	
420	KLB607		490	KLB709	22.4.58	560	KGU10	
421	KLB608		491	KLB710	27.2.58	561	KGU11	
422	KLB609		492	KLB711		562	KGU12	
423	KLB610	13.1.61	493	KXW277		563	KGU13	
424	KLB611		494	KXW278		564	KGU14	
425	KLB612		495	KXW279		565	KGU15	
426	KLB613		496	KXW280		566	KGU16	
427	KLB614		497	KXW281		567	KGU17	
428	KLB615		498	KXW282		568	KGU18	
429	KLB616		499	KXW283		569	KGU19	
430	KLB617		500	KXW284		570	KGU20	
431	KLB618		501	JXC20	15.7.58	571	KGU21	
432	KLB619		502	KXW285		572	KGU22	
433	KLB620	13.1.61	503	KXW286		573	KGU23	
434	KLB621		504	KXW287		574	KGU24	
435	KLB622		505	KXW288		575	KGU25	
436	KLB623		506	KXW289		576	KGU26	

RTL		Date out of stock	RTL		Date out of stock	RTL		Date out of stock
577	KGU27		647	KGU97		717	KXW67	
578	KGU28		648	KGU98		718	KXW68	
579	KGU29		649	KGU99		719	KXW69	
580	KGU30		650	KGU100		720	KXW70	
581	KGU31		651	KXW1		721	KXW71	
582	KGU32		652	KXW2		722	KXW72	
583	KGU33		653	KXW3		723	KXW73	
584	KGU34		654	KXW4		724	KXW74	
585	KGU35		655	KXW5		725	KXW75	
586	KGU36		656	KXW6		726	KXW76	
587	KGU37		657	KXW7		727	KXW77	
588	KGU38		658	KXW8		728	KXW78	
589	KGU39		659	KXW9		729	KXW79	
590	KGU40		660	KXW10		730	KXW80	
591	KGU41		661	KXW11		731	KXW81	
592	KGU42		662	KXW12		732	KXW82	
593	KGU43		663	KXW13		733	KXW83	
594	KGU44		664	KXW14		734	KXW84	
595	KGU45		665	KXW15		735	KXW85	
596	KGU46		666	KXW16		736	KXW86	
597	KGU47		667	KXW17		737	KXW87	
598	KGU48		668	KXW18		738	KXW88	
599	KGU49		669	KXW19		739	KXW89	
600	KGU50		670	KXW20		740	KXW90	
601	KGU51		671	KXW21		741	KXW91	
602	KGU52		672	KXW22		742	KXW92	
603	KGU53		673	KXW23		743	KXW93	
604	KGU54		674	KXW24		744	KXW94	
605	KGU55		675	KXW25		745	KXW95	
606	KGU56		676	KXW26		746	KXW96	
607	KGU57		677	KXW27		747	KXW97	
608	KGU58		678	KXW28		748	KXW98	
609	KGU59		679	KXW29		749	KXW99	
610	KGU60		680	KXW30		750	KXW100	
611	KGU61		681	KXW31		751	KYY721	
612	KGU62		682	KXW32		752	KYY722	
613	KGU63		683	KXW33		753	KYY723	
614	KGU64		684	KXW34		754	KYY724	
615	KGU65		685	KXW35		755	KYY725	
616	KGU66		686	KXW36		756	KYY726	
617	KGU67		687	KXW37		757	KYY727	
618	KGU68		688	KXW38		758	KYY728	
619	KGU69		689	KXW39		759	KYY729	
620	KGU70		690	KXW40		760	KYY730	
621	KGU71		691	KXW41		761	KYY731	
622	KGU72		692	KXW42		762	KYY732	
623	KGU73		693	KXW43		763	KYY733	
624	KGU74		694	KXW44		764	KYY734	
625	KGU75		695	KXW45		765	KYY735	
626	KGU76		696	KXW46		766	KYY736	
627	KGU77		697	KXW47		767	KYY737	
628	KGU78		698	KXW48		768	KYY738	
629	KGU79		699	KXW49		769	KYY739	
630	KGU80		700	KXW50		770	KYY740	
631	KGU81		701	KXW51		771	KYY741	
632	KGU82		702	KXW52		772	KYY742	
633	KGU83		703	KXW53		773	KYY743	
634	KGU84		704	KXW54		774	KYY744	
635	KGU85		705	KXW55		775	KYY745	
636	KGU86		706	KXW56		776	KYY746	
637	KGU87		707	KXW57		777	KYY747	
638	KGU88		708	KXW58		778	KYY748	
639	KGU89		709	KXW59		779	KYY749	
640	KGU90		710	KXW60		780	KYY750	
641	KGU91		711	KXW61		781	KYY751	
642	KGU92		712	KXW62		782	KYY752	
643	KGU93		713	KXW63		783	KYY753	
644	KGU94		714	KXW64		784	KYY754	
645	KGU95		715	KXW65		785	KYY755	
646	KGU96		716	KXW66		786	KYY756	

RTL

787	KYY757	857	LLU847	927	LLU917
788	KYY758	858	LLU848	928	LLU918
789	KYY759	859	LLU849	929	LLU919
790	KYY760	860	LLU850	930	LLU920
791	KYY761	861	LLU851	931	LLU921
792	KYY762	862	LLU852	992	LLU922
793	KYY763	863	LLU853	933	LLU923
794	KYY764	864	LLU854	934	LLU924
795	KYY765	865	LLU855	935	LLU925
796	KYY766	866	LLU856	936	LLU926
797	KYY767	867	LLU857	937	LLU927
798	KYY768	868	LLU858	938	LLU928
799	KYY769	869	LLU859	939	LLU929
800	KYY770	870	LLU860	940	LLU930
801	KYY771	871	LLU861	941	LLU931
802	KYY772	872	LLU862	942	LLU932
803	KYY773	873	LLU863	943	LLU933
804	KYY774	874	LLU864	944	LLU934
805	KYY775	875	LLU865	945	LLU935
806	KYY776	876	LLU866	946	LLU936
807	KYY777	877	LLU867	947	LLU937
808	KYY778	878	LLU868	948	LLU938
809	KYY779	879	LLU869	949	LLU939
810	KYY780	880	LLU870	950	LLU940
811	KYY781	881	LLU871	951	LUC326
812	KYY782	882	LLU872	952	LUC327
813	KYY783	883	LLU873	953	LUC328
814	KYY784	884	LLU874	954	LUC329
815	KYY785	885	LLU875	955	LUC330
816	KYY786	886	LLU876	956	LUC331
817	KYY787	887	LLU877	957	LUC332
818	KYY788	888	LLU878	958	LUC333
819	KYY789	889	LLU879	959	LUC334
820	KYY790	890	LLU880	960	LUC335
821	KYY791	891	LLU881	961	LUC336
822	KYY792	892	LLU882	962	LUC337
823	KYY793	893	LLU883	963	LUC338
824	KYY794	894	LLU884	964	LUC339
825	KYY795	895	LLU885	965	LUC340
826	KYY796	896	LLU886	966	LUC341
827	KYY797	897	LLU887	967	LUC342
828	KYY798	898	LLU888	968	LUC343
829	KYY799	899	LLU889	969	LUC344
830	KYY800	900	LLU890	970	LUC345
831	KYY801	901	LLU891	971	LUC346
832	KYY802	902	LLU892	972	LUC347
833	KYY803	903	LLU893	973	LUC348
834	KYY804	904	LLU894	974	LUC349
835	KYY805	905	LLU895	975	LUC350
836	KYY806	906	LLU896	976	LUC351
837	KYY807	907	LLU897	977	LUC352
838	KYY808	908	LLU898	978	LUC353
839	KYY809	909	LLU899	979	LUC354
840	KYY810	910	LLU900	980	LUC355
841	KYY811	911	LLU901	981	LUC356
842	KYY812	912	LLU902	982	LUC357
843	KYY813	913	LLU903	983	LUC358
844	KYY814	914	LLU904	984	LUC359
845	KYY815	915	LLU905	985	LUC360
846	KYY816	916	LLU906	986	LUC361
847	KYY817	917	LLU907	987	LUC362
848	KYY818	918	LLU908	988	LUC363
849	KYY819	919	LLU909	989	LUC364
850	KYY820	920	LLU910	990	LUC365
851	LLU841	921	LLU911	991	LUC366
852	LLU842	922	LLU912	992	LUC367
853	LLU843	923	LLU913	993	LUC368
854	LLU844	924	LLU914	994	LUC369
855	LLU845	925	LLU915	995	LUC370
856	LLU846	926	LLU916	996	LUC371

RTL		Date out of stock	RTL		Date out of stock	RTL	
997	LUC372		1067	LUC74		1137	LYF61
998	LUC373		1068	LUC75	13.1.61	1138	LYF62
999	LUC374		1069	LUC76		1139	LYF63
1000	LUC375		1070	LUC77		1140	LYF64
1001	KYY644		1071	LUC78		1141	LYF65
1002	KYY645		1072	LUC79		1142	LYF66
1003	KYY646		1073	LUC250		1143	LYF67
1004	KYY647		1074	LUC251		1144	LYF68
1005	KYY648		1075	LUC252		1145	LYF69
1006	KYY649		1076	LUC253		1146	LYF70
1007	KYY705		1077	LUC254		1147	LYF71
1008	KYY706	22.4.58	1078	LUC255		1148	LYF89
1009	KYY707		1079	LUC256		1149	LYF90
1010	KYY708		1080	LUC257		1150	LYF91
1011	KYY709		1081	LUC258		1151	LYF92
1012	KYY710		1082	LUC259		1152	LYF93
1013	KYY711		1083	LUC260		1153	LYF94
1014	KYY712		1084	LUC261		1154	LYF95
1015	KYY713		1085	LUC262		1155	LYF96
1016	KYY714		1086	LUC263		1156	LYF97
1017	KYY715	13.1.61	1087	LUC264		1157	LYF98
1018	LLU772		1088	LUC265		1158	LYF99
1019	LLU773		1089	LUC282		1159	LYF100
1020	LLU774		1090	LUC283		1160	LYF101
1021	LLU775		1091	LUC284		1161	LYF102
1022	LLU776		1092	LUC285		1162	LYF103
1023	LLU777		1093	LUC286		1163	LYF104
1024	LLU778		1094	LUC287		1164	LYF105
1025	LLU779		1095	LUC305		1165	LYF106
1026	LLU780		1096	LUC306		1166	LYF107
1027	LLU781		1097	LUC307		1167	LYF108
1028	LLU782		1098	LUC308		1168	LYF109
1029	LLU783	13.1.61	1099	LUC309		1169	LYF110
1030	LLU784		1100	LUC310		1170	LYF111
1031	LLU785		1101	LUC311		1171	LYF112
1032	LLU786		1102	LUC312		1172	LYF113
1033	LLU787		1103	LUC313		1173	LYF114
1034	LLU788		1104	LUC314		1174	LYF115
1035	LLU789		1105	LUC315		1175	LYF116
1036	LLU790		1106	LUC316		1176	LYF117
1037	LLU791		1107	LUC317		1177	LYF118
1038	LLU792		1108	LUC318		1178	LYF119
1039	LLU793		1109	LUC319		1179	LYF120
1040	LLU819		1110	LYF34		1180	LYF121
1041	LLU820		1111	LYF35		1181	LYF122
1042	LLU821	13.1.61	1112	LYF36		1182	LYF123
1043	LLU822		1113	LYF37		1183	LYF124
1044	LLU823		1114	LYF38		1184	LYF125
1045	LLU824		1115	LYF39		1185	LYF126
1046	LLU825		1116	LYF40		1186	LYF127
1047	LLU826		1117	LYF41		1187	LYF128
1048	LLU827		1118	LYF42		1188	LYF129
1049	LLU828		1119	LYF43		1189	LYF130
1050	LLU829		1120	LYF44		1190	LYF131
1051	LLU830		1121	LYF45		1191	LYF132
1052	LUC23		1122	LYF46		1192	LYF133
1053	LUC24		1123	LYF47		1193	LYF134
1054	LUC25		1124	LYF48		1194	LYF135
1055	LUC26		1125	LYF49		1195	LYF136
1056	LUC27		1126	LYF50		1196	LYF137
1057	LUC28		1127	LYF51		1197	LYF138
1058	LUC41		1128	LYF52		1198	LYF139
1059	LUC42		1129	LYF53		1199	LYF140
1060	LUC43		1130	LYF54		1200	LYF141
1061	LUC68		1131	LYF55		1201	LYF142
1062	LUC69		1132	LYF56		1202	LYF143
1063	LUC70		1133	LYF57		1203	LYF144
1064	LUC71		1134	LYF58		1204	LYF145
1065	LUC72		1135	LYF59		1205	LYF146
1066	LUC73		1136	LYF60		1206	LYF147

RTL		Date out of stock	RTL		Date out of stock	RTL		Date out of stock
1207	LYF148		1278	LYR810		1349	MXX72	5.12.58
1208	LYF149		1279	LYR811		1350	MXX73	
1209	LYF150	19.7.62	1280	LYR812		1351	MXX74	
1210	LYF151		1281	LYR813		1352	MXX75	
1211	LYF152		1282	LYR814		1353	MXX76	
1212	LYF153		1283	LYR815		1354	MXX77	
1213	LYF154		1284	LYR816		1355	MXX78	
1214	LYF155		1285	LYR817		1356	MXX79	
1215	LYF156		1286	LYR818		1357	MXX80	
1216	LYF157		1287	LYR819		1358	MXX81	
1217	LYF158		1288	LYR820		1359	MXX82	9.3.59
1218	LYF159		1289	LYR821		1360	MXX83	
1219	LYF160		1290	LYR822		1361	MXX84	
1220	LYF161		1291	LYR823		1362	MXX85	
1221	LYF162		1292	LYR824		1363	MXX86	
1222	LYF163		1293	LYR825		1364	MXX87	
1223	LYF164		1294	LYR828		1365	MXX88	
1224	LYF165		1295	LYR829		1366	MXX89	
1225	LYF166		1296	LYR830		1367	MXX90	
1226	LYF167		1297	LYR831		1368	MXX91	
1227	LYR759		1298	LYR832		1369	MXX92	9.3.59
1228	LYR760		1299	LYR833		1370	MXX93	
1229	LYR761		1300	LYR834		1371	MXX94	
1230	LYR762		1301	LYR835		1372	MXX95	
1231	LYR763		1302	LYR936		1373	MXX96	
1232	LYR764		1303	LYR937		1374	MXX97	
1233	LYR765		1304	LYR938		1375	MXX98	
1234	LYR766		1305	LYR939		1376	MXX99	
1235	LYR767		1306	LYR940		1377	MXX100	9.3.59
1236	LYR768		1307	LYR935		1378	MXX101	
1237	LYR769		1308	LYR956		1379	MXX102	
1238	LYR770		1309	LYR957		1380	MXX103	
1239	LYR771		1310	LYR958		1381	MXX104	
1240	LYR772		1311	LYR959		1382	MXX105	
1241	LYR773		1312	LYR960		1383	MXX106	
1242	LYR774		1313	LYR961		1384	MXX107	
1243	LYR775		1314	MLL676		1385	MXX108	
1244	LYR776		1315	MLL677		1386	MXX109	
1245	LYR777		1316	MLL678		1387	MXX110	
1246	LYR778		1317	MLL679		1388	MXX111	
1247	LYR779		1318	MLL680		1389	MXX112	
1248	LYR780		1319	MLL681		1390	MXX113	
1249	LYR781		1320	MLL682		1391	MXX114	
1250	LYR782		1321	MLL683		1392	MXX115	
1251	LYR783		1322	MLL684		1393	MXX116	
1252	LYR784		1323	MLL685		1394	MXX117	
1253	LYR785		1324	MLL686		1395	MXX118	
1254	LYR786		1325	MLL687		1396	MXX119	
1255	LYR787		1326	MLL697		1397	MXX120	
1256	LYR788	5.9.62	1327	MLL698		1398	MXX121	
1257	LYR789		1328	MLL699		1399	MXX122	
1258	LYR790		1329	MLL700		1400	MXX123	
1259	LYR791		1330	MLL701		1401	MXX124	
1260	LYR792		1331	MLL702		1402	MXX125	
1261	LYR793		1332	MLL703		1403	MXX126	20.3.59
1262	LYR794		1333	MXX32		1404	MXX127	
1263	LYR795		1334	MXX33		1405	MXX128	
1264	LYR796		1335	MXX34		1406	MXX129	
1265	LYR797		1336	MXX35		1407	MXX130	
1266	LYR798		1337	OLD813		1408	MXX215	
1267	LYR799		1338	MXX61		1409	MXX216	
1268	LYR800		1339	MXX62		1410	MXX217	
1269	LYR801		1340	MXX63		1411	MXX218	
1270	LYR802		1341	MXX64		1412	MXX219	
1271	LYR803		1342	MXX65		1413	MXX220	9.3.59
1272	LYR804		1343	MXX66		1414	NLE501	
1273	LYR805		1344	MXX67		1415	NLE502	
1274	LYR806		1345	MXX68		1416	NLE503	
1275	LYR807		1346	MXX69		1417	NLE504	
1276	LYR808		1347	MXX70		1418	NLE505	
1277	LYR809		1348	MXX71	6.3.59	1419	NLE506	

RTL		Date out of stock	RTL		Date out of stock	RTL		Date out of stock
1420	NLE507		1491	OLD600		1562	OLD781	
1421	NLE508		1492	OLD601	24.8.59	1563	OLD782	
1422	NLE509		1493	OLD602		1564	OLD783	
1423	NLE510		1494	OLD603	24.8.59	1565	OLD784	
1424	NLE511		1495	OLD604		1566	OLD785	
1425	NLE512		1496	OLD605		1567	OLD786	
1426	NLE513		1497	OLD606	22.4.58	1568	OLD787	
1427	NLE701		1498	OLD607		1569	OLD788	
1428	NLE702		1499	OLD608		1570	OLD789	
1429	NLE703		1500	OLD609		1571	OLD790	
1430	NLE704		1501	OLD610		1572	OLD791	
1431	NLE705	21.4.59	1502	OLD611		1573	OLD792	
1432	NLE706		1503	OLD612		1574	OLD793	
1433	NLE707		1504	OLD613		1575	OLD794	
1434	NLE708	9.3.59	1505	OLD614	6.3.59	1576	OLD795	
1435	NLE709		1506	OLD615		1577	OLD796	
1436	NLE710		1507	OLD616		1578	OLD797	
1437	NLE711		1508	OLD617		1579	OLD798	
1438	NLE712		1509	OLD618		1580	OLD799	
1439	NLE713	9.3.59	1510	OLD619	22.4.58	1581	OLD800	4.11.58
1440	NLE714		1511	OLD620		1582	OLD801	
1441	NLE715		1512	OLD621		1583	OLD802	
1442	NLE716		1513	OLD622		1584	OLD803	
1443	NLE717		1514	OLD623		1585	OLD804	
1444	NLE718	18.3.59	1515	OLD624	6.3.59	1586	OLD805	
1445	NLE719		1516	OLD625		1587	OLD806	
1446	NLE720		1517	OLD626		1588	OLD807	
1447	NLE721		1518	OLD627		1589	OLD808	
1448	NLE722		1519	OLD628		1590	OLD809	
1449	NLE723		1520	OLD629		1591	OLD810	
1450	NLE724	24.8.59	1521	OLD630		1592	OLD811	
1451	NLE725		1522	OLD631		1593	OLD812	
1452	NLE726		1523	OLD632		1594	OLD814	
1453	NLE727		1524	OLD633		1595	OLD815	
1454	NLE728		1525	OLD634		1596	OLD816	
1455	NLE729		1526	OLD635		1597	OLD817	
1456	NLE730		1527	OLD636	22.4.58	1598	OLD818	
1457	NLE731		1528	OLD637		1599	OLD819	
1458	NLE732		1529	OLD638		1600	OLD820	
1459	NLE733		1530	OLD639		1601	OLD536	
1460	NLE734		1531	OLD640		1602	OLD831	
1461	NLE735		1532	OLD641		1603	OLD832	
1462	NLE736		1533	OLD642		1604	OLD833	
1463	NLE737		1534	OLD643		1605	OLD834	
1464	NLE738	14.3.59	1535	OLD644		1606	OLD835	
1465	NLE739		1536	OLD645		1607	OLD836	
1466	NLE751	9.3.59	1537	OLD646		1608	OLD837	
1467	NLE752		1538	OLD647	22.4.58	1609	OLD838	
1468	NLE753		1539	OLD648		1610	OLD839	
1469	NXP955		1540	OLD649		1611	OLD840	
1470	NXP956	24.8.59	1541	OLD650		1612	OLD841	
1471	NXP957		1542	OLD651		1613	OLD842	
1472	NXP958	9.3.59	1543	OLD652		1614	OLD843	
1473	NXP959		1544	OLD653		1615	OLD844	
1474	NXP960		1545	OLD654		1616	OLD845	
1475	OLD571		1546	OLD655		1617	OLD846	
1476	OLD572		1547	OLD656		1618	OLD847	
1477	OLD573		1548	OLD657		1619	OLD848	
1478	OLD574		1549	OLD658		1620	OLD849	
1479	OLD575		1550	OLD659		1621	OLD850	
1480	OLD576		1551	OLD660		1622	OLD851	
1481	OLD590		1552	OLD661		1623	OLD852	
1482	OLD591		1553	OLD662		1624	OLD853	
1483	OLD592		1554	OLD663		1625	OLD854	
1484	OLD593		1555	OLD664		1626	OLD855	
1485	OLD594		1556	OLD665		1627	OLD856	
1486	OLD595		1557	OLD666		1628	OLD857	
1487	OLD596	24.8.59	1558	OLD777		1629	OLD858	
1488	OLD597		1559	OLD778		1630	OLD859	
1489	OLD598		1560	OLD779		1631	OLD860	
1490	OLD599	22.4.58	1561	OLD780				

The neater arrangement of the double front advertisements and the rubber mounted glazing of the indicator boxes were two guides to the identity of the 6RT6 all-Leyland RTW class, although the extra six inches of width compared with an RTL was also fairly obvious. RTW 315 is parked in the trolleybus turning circle on the Finchley Road side of Golders Green station on one of Tottenham's Saturday only runnings on route 102.
Capital Transport Collection

RTW

The manufacturing agreement with Leyland in 1947 included five hundred eight-foot wide Titans, modified in the same way as the RTLs. The bodywork was supplied by Leyland, using their standard metal framed construction but modified to resemble the standard RT3/1 design. RTW 1 went into service at Tottenham garage in May 1949 and the whole class was in service by December 1950. These were London's first 8ft wide motor buses and were at first restricted to specifically approved suburban routes. Following a series of tests in 1950 during which all routes serving Notting Hill Gate, then Shaftesbury Avenue and finally Threadneedle Street were converted temporarily to RTW, agreement was secured for them to operate in central London, although still subject to specific route approval. Transfers onto central area routes took place from May 1951 and eventually the majority were so allocated. Only two of the class have been overseas. RTWs 421 and 422 visited Berlin for the British Industries Fair in September/October 1950, making a journey through communist East Germany. At the end of 1962 all 500 were still in service.

The RTWs were fitted with flashing trafficators in 1959/1960 and with the same modified rear arrow arrangement as on the RTs in 1962.

Walworth garage received its first RTWs from those made surplus by the service cuts which followed the 1958 bus strike, bringing the class in bulk to the streets of inner south London for the first time. RTW 460 is on the stand in the centre of Exhibition Road at South Kensington station. G. Mead

Clearly showing the difference in width between the standard RT/RTL body and the RTW, this view of RTL 635 and RTW 76 at the top of Tottenham Court Road also shows the flashing trafficators fitted in 1959/60. F.W. Ivey

Chassis: Leyland Titan 6RT
Engine: Leyland O600 six-cylinder 9.8 litre oil 125 bhp (derated to 115bhp)
Transmission: AEC D140 4-speed air operated preselective with fluid flywheel
Bodywork: Leyland
Capacity: H56R
L.T. code: 6RT6
Built: 1949–50
Number built: 500
Number in stock: 1.1.55: 500   31.12.62: 500

RTW

#		#		#		#		#	
1	KGK501	58	KGK558	115	KGK615	172	KLB902	229	KLB959
2	KGK502	59	KGK559	116	KGK616	173	KLB903	230	KLB960
3	KGK503	60	KGK560	117	KGK617	174	KLB904	231	KLB961
4	KGK504	61	KGK561	118	KGK618	175	KLB905	232	KLB962
5	KGK505	62	KGK562	119	KGK619	176	KLB906	233	KLB963
6	KGK506	63	KGK563	120	KGK620	177	KLB907	234	KLB964
7	KGK507	64	KGK564	121	KGK621	178	KLB908	235	KLB965
8	KGK508	65	KGK565	122	KGK622	179	KLB909	236	KLB966
9	KGK509	66	KGK566	123	KGK623	180	KLB910	237	KLB967
10	KGK510	67	KGK567	124	KGK624	181	KLB911	238	KLB968
11	KGK511	68	KGK568	125	KGK625	182	KLB912	239	KLB969
12	KGK512	69	KGK569	126	KGK626	183	KLB913	240	KLB970
13	KGK513	70	KGK570	127	KGK627	184	KLB914	241	KLB971
14	KGK514	71	KGK571	128	KGK628	185	KLB915	242	KLB972
15	KGK515	72	KGK572	129	KGK629	186	KLB916	243	KLB973
16	KGK516	73	KGK573	130	KGK630	187	KLB917	244	KLB974
17	KGK517	74	KGK574	131	KGK631	188	KLB918	245	KLB975
18	KGK518	75	KGK575	132	KGK632	189	KLB919	246	KLB976
19	KGK519	76	KGK576	133	KGK633	190	KLB920	247	KLB977
20	KGK520	77	KGK577	134	KGK634	191	KLB921	248	KLB978
21	KGK521	78	KGK578	135	KGK635	192	KLB922	249	KLB979
22	KGK522	79	KGK579	136	KGK636	193	KLB923	250	KLB980
23	KGK523	80	KGK580	137	KGK637	194	KLB924	251	KXW351
24	KGK524	81	KGK581	138	KGK638	195	KLB925	252	KXW352
25	KGK525	82	KGK582	139	KGK639	196	KLB926	253	KXW353
26	KGK526	83	KGK583	140	KGK640	197	KLB927	254	KXW354
27	KGK527	84	KGK584	141	KGK641	198	KLB928	255	KXW355
28	KGK528	85	KGK585	142	KGK642	199	KLB929	256	KXW356
29	KGK529	86	KGK586	143	KGK643	200	KLB930	257	KXW357
30	KGK530	87	KGK587	144	KGK644	201	KLB931	258	KXW358
31	KGK531	88	KGK588	145	KGK645	202	KLB932	259	KXW359
32	KGK532	89	KGK589	146	KGK646	203	KLB933	260	KXW360
33	KGK533	90	KGK590	147	KGK647	204	KLB934	261	KXW361
34	KGK534	91	KGK591	148	KGK648	205	KLB935	262	KXW362
35	KGK535	92	KGK592	149	KGK649	206	KLB936	263	KXW363
36	KGK536	93	KGK593	150	KGK650	207	KLB937	264	KXW364
37	KGK537	94	KGK594	151	KLB881	208	KLB938	265	KXW365
38	KGK538	95	KGK595	152	KLB882	209	KLB939	266	KXW366
39	KGK539	96	KGK596	153	KLB883	210	KLB940	267	KXW367
40	KGK540	97	KGK597	154	KLB884	211	KLB941	268	KXW368
41	KGK541	98	KGK598	155	KLB885	212	KLB942	269	KXW369
42	KGK542	99	KGK599	156	KLB886	213	KLB943	270	KXW370
43	KGK543	100	KGK600	157	KLB887	214	KLB944	271	KXW371
44	KGK544	101	KGK601	158	KLB888	215	KLB945	272	KXW372
45	KGK545	102	KGK602	159	KLB889	216	KLB946	273	KXW373
46	KGK546	103	KGK603	160	KLB890	217	KLB947	274	KXW374
47	KGK547	104	KGK604	161	KLB891	218	KLB948	275	KXW375
48	KGK548	105	KGK605	162	KLB892	219	KLB949	276	KXW376
49	KGK549	106	KGK606	163	KLB893	220	KLB950	277	KXW377
50	KGK550	107	KGK607	164	KLB894	221	KLB951	278	KXW378
51	KGK551	108	KGK608	165	KLB895	222	KLB952	279	KXW379
52	KGK552	109	KGK609	166	KLB896	223	KLB953	280	KXW380
53	KGK553	110	KGK610	167	KLB897	224	KLB954	281	KXW381
54	KGK554	111	KGK611	168	KLB898	225	KLB955	282	KXW382
55	KGK555	112	KGK612	169	KLB899	226	KLB956	283	KXW383
56	KGK556	113	KGK613	170	KLB900	227	KLB957	284	KXW384
57	KGK557	114	KGK614	171	KLB901	228	KLB958	285	KXW385

RTW   RTW   RTW   RTW   RTW

#	Reg	#	Reg	#	Reg	#	Reg	#	Reg
286	KXW386	329	KXW429	372	LLU522	415	LLU565	458	LLU948
287	KXW387	330	KXW430	373	LLU523	416	LLU566	459	LLU949
288	KXW388	331	KXW431	374	LLU524	417	LLU567	460	LLU950
289	KXW389	332	KXW432	375	LLU525	418	LLU568	461	LLU951
290	KXW390	333	KXW433	376	LLU526	419	LLU569	462	LLU952
291	KXW391	334	KXW434	377	LLU527	420	LLU570	463	LLU953
292	KXW392	335	KXW435	378	LLU528	421	LLU571	464	LLU954
293	KXW393	336	KXW436	379	LLU529	422	LLU572	465	LLU955
294	KXW394	337	KXW437	380	LLU530	423	LLU573	466	LLU956
295	KXW395	338	KXW438	381	LLU531	424	LLU574	467	LLU957
296	KXW396	339	KXW439	382	LLU532	425	LLU575	468	LLU958
297	KXW397	340	KXW440	383	LLU533	426	LLU576	469	LLU959
298	KXW398	341	KXW441	384	LLU534	427	LLU577	470	LLU960
299	KXW399	342	KXW442	385	LLU535	428	LLU578	471	LLU961
300	KXW400	343	KXW443	386	LLU536	429	LLU579	472	LLU962
301	KXW401	344	KXW444	387	LLU537	430	LLU580	473	LLU963
302	KXW402	345	KXW445	388	LLU538	431	LLU581	474	LLU964
303	KXW403	346	KXW446	389	LLU539	432	LLU582	475	LLU965
304	KXW404	347	KXW447	390	LLU540	433	LLU583	476	LLU966
305	KXW405	348	KXW448	391	LLU541	434	LLU584	477	LLU967
306	KXW406	349	KXW449	392	LLU542	435	LLU585	478	LLU968
307	KXW407	350	KXW450	393	LLU543	436	LLU586	479	LLU969
308	KXW408	351	LLU501	394	LLU544	437	LLU587	480	LLU970
309	KXW409	352	LLU502	395	LLU545	438	LLU588	481	LLU971
310	KXW410	353	LLU503	396	LLU546	439	LLU589	482	LLU972
311	KXW411	354	LLU504	397	LLU547	440	LLU590	483	LLU973
312	KXW412	355	LLU505	398	LLU548	441	LLU591	484	LLU974
313	KXW413	356	LLU506	399	LLU549	442	LLU592	485	LLU975
314	KXW414	357	LLU507	400	LLU550	443	LLU593	486	LLU976
315	KXW415	358	LLU508	401	LLU551	444	LLU594	487	LLU977
316	KXW416	359	LLU509	402	LLU552	445	LLU595	488	LLU978
317	KXW417	360	LLU510	403	LLU553	446	LLU596	489	LLU979
318	KXW418	361	LLU511	404	LLU554	447	LLU597	490	LLU980
319	KXW419	362	LLU512	405	LLU555	448	LLU598	491	LLU981
320	KXW420	363	LLU513	406	LLU556	449	LLU599	492	LLU982
321	KXW421	364	LLU514	407	LLU557	450	LLU600	493	LLU983
322	KXW422	365	LLU515	408	LLU558	451	LLU941	494	LLU984
323	KXW423	366	LLU516	409	LLU559	452	LLU942	495	LLU985
324	KXW424	367	LLU517	410	LLU560	453	LLU943	496	LLU986
325	KXW425	368	LLU518	411	LLU561	454	LLU944	497	LLU987
326	KXW426	369	LLU519	412	LLU562	455	LLU945	498	LLU988
327	KXW427	370	LLU520	413	LLU563	456	LLU946	499	LLU989
328	KXW428	371	LLU521	414	LLU564	457	LLU947	500	LLU990

RTC

RTC 1 was intended as a prototype for the large fleet of double-deck Green Line coaches which was planned as part of the post-war vehicle replacement programme. It was not a new bus but a heavily modified 2RT2. RT 97 was one of the first production batch of RTs and was built in April 1940. It suffered bomb damage during the war and was one of the buses chosen for Pay-As-You-Enter experiments in 1946. On completion of these experiments, it was taken into the experimental shop at Chiswick Works and extensively rebuilt. The modified vehicle had a low full width downward sloping bonnet incorporating the nearside wing. There was an oblong chromium finished grille but the radiator itself was transferred to a position under the stairs. Opening windows were of the single piece type but could be opened only half way. Interior decor was predominantly green with cream window cappings and ceiling panels. Experimental 'airline standard' seats of a new design with 'Dunlopillo' filled squabs were loosely covered in a new design of moquette. Fluorescent saloon and indicator lighting was fitted to a London bus for the first time. RTC 1 operated experimentally from 6th April 1949 on routes 715, 711, 708 and 704 but was relegated to bus work at Leatherhead garage in December. It was withdrawn from service in March 1953 and used for some time in heating development trials at Chiswick. It was sold to W. North of Leeds in March 1955 and then ran for some years as a staff transport for Vernon's Pools of Liverpool.

Chassis:	AEC Regent III 0661
Engine:	AEC A185B 6-cylinder 9.6 litre direct injection 125 bhp (derated to 115 bhp)
Transmission:	AEC D140 four speed air operated preselective with fluid flywheel
Bodywork:	LPTB rebuilt by LTE
Capacity:	H26/20RD
L.T. code:	5RT5
Built:	1940 (as RT 97) rebuilt 1949
Number built:	1
Number in stock: 1.1.55: 1	Out of stock: 14.3.55

RTC	Date out of stock
1 FXT272	14.3.55

SRT

Deliveries of standard RT family buses to London Transport in the early post-war years were slow to get under way and the availability of bodies and chassis frequently did not match. To overcome a temporary excess of body building over chassis building capacity, London Transport decided to modify the chassis frames of 300 pre-war STLs to enable them to be mounted with standard RT family bodywork. The mechanical specification remained unchanged. The first SRTs went into service in April 1949 but proved to be unsatisfactory in service because the extra weight made them sluggish and, most crucially, caused the brakes to be inadequate. Modifications were made to the braking system but production was halted after the first 160 and the buses were relegated to second line duties wherever possible. They were withdrawn in 1954 and their bodies transferred to new RT chassis but fifteen chassis were retained as slaves to carry works float bodies, stored at New Cross garage, pending the full introduction of the flow overhaul system at Aldenham in June 1955.

Chassis:	AEC Regent 0661 rebuilt by London Transport
Engine:	AEC A173 6-cylinder 7.7 litre direct injection 95bhp oil
Transmission:	AEC D132 direct selection preselective with fluid flywheel
Bodywork:	Park Royal
Capacity:	H30/26R
L.T. code:	8RT9 (49–125) or 1/8RT9
Built:	1949
Number built:	160
Number in stock:	1.1.55: 16 (chassis only) Last out of stock: 17.8.55

SRT		Date out of stock	SRT		Date out of stock	SRT		Date out of stock
49	FJJ751	15.6.55	138	EGO463	27.6.55	146	DLU84	23.6.55
83	FXT95	8.7.55	139	DLU100	12.7.55	148	ELP126	17.8.55
84	FJJ682	9.6.55	140	EGO466	8.8.55	154	DLU54	17.8.55
114	FJJ714	4.8.55	141	EGO488	8.7.55	158	DYL110	9.8.55
115	FJJ724	11.7.55	143	ELP171	23.6.55			
125	FXT91	8.7.55	144	DLU60	8.8.55			

The two batches of RLHs were virtually identical in appearance, the only difference being the use of chromium plated radiator shells on the first batch but polished aluminium on the 1952 batch. Green RLH 12, a 1RLH1, is at Onslow Street bus station, Guildford. John Gillham

RLH

London Transport's fleet of lowbridge buses was always small but LT had intended designing a post-war replacement which would also have been suitable to operate through Blackwall Tunnel. This plan was abandoned when the Road Transport Executive of the British Transport Commission offered London Transport twenty lowbridge AEC Regents which were surplus to the requirements of the newly acquired Midland General Omnibus Co. in 1950. These were standard 'provincial' versions of the Regent III very similar in specification to the RT but differing in a number of details. The differences included a higher bonnet line and deeper chromium plated radiator shell. The dynamo was driven by the engine, rather than the propeller shaft and this caused a bulge in the bonnet side. The fifty-three seat body was also a standard Weymann product, similar in basic design to the 18STL20s. All twenty buses were painted green and were used to replace STs and to expand services in the Country Area.

The remaining pre-war and wartime lowbridge buses were replaced by a further batch of fifty-six almost identical RLHs in 1952. The chassis of these were the later 9613E model designed for 27 foot long bodywork but the RLHs were built to the old standard of 26 feet. They also had polished aluminium radiator shells. RLH 21–53 were painted green for Country Bus use; the remainder were red. At the end of 1962, all seventy-six were still in service.

The RLHs were fitted with flashing trafficators in 1959/1960 and the Country Bus vehicles with saloon heaters between 1961 and 1963.

Twenty-three of the 1952 batch of lowbridge Regent IIIs were painted red for use on routes 127 and 230 but service cuts in 1955 released enough for routes 248 and 249 to be included and, when route 127 became a casualty of the 1958 strike, the released RLHs were used to replace single-deck 208A by lowbridge route 178. RLH 29, having the later 9613E chassis was a 2RLH1/2, and was photographed at Clapton Pond in September 1960.
Capital Transport Collection

Chassis:	AEC Regent III 9612E (1–20); 9613E (21–76)
Engine:	AEC A208 6-cylinder 9.6 litre 125 bhp (derated to 115 bhp)
Transmission:	AEC D140 4-speed air operated preselective with fluid flywheel
Bodywork:	Weymann
Capacity:	L53R
L.T. code:	1RLH1 (1–20); 2RLH1/1 (21–76)
Built:	1950 (1–20); 1952 (21–76)
Number built:	76
Number in stock:	1.1.55: 76 31.12.62: 76

RLH

	RLH		RLH		RLH		RLH		RLH
1	KYY501	17	KYY517	33	MXX233	49	MXX249	65	MXX265
2	KYY502	18	KYY518	34	MXX234	50	MXX250	66	MXX266
3	KYY503	19	KYY519	35	MXX235	51	MXX251	67	MXX267
4	KYY504	20	KYY520	36	MXX236	52	MXX252	68	MXX268
5	KYY505	21	MXX221	37	MXX237	53	MXX253	69	MXX269
6	KYY506	22	MXX222	38	MXX238	54	MXX254	70	MXX270
7	KYY507	23	MXX223	39	MXX239	55	MXX255	71	MXX271
8	KYY508	24	MXX224	40	MXX240	56	MXX256	72	MXX272
9	KYY509	25	MXX225	41	MXX241	57	MXX257	73	MXX273
10	KYY510	26	MXX226	42	MXX242	58	MXX258	74	MXX274
11	KYY511	27	MXX227	43	MXX243	59	MXX259	75	MXX275
12	KYY512	28	MXX228	44	MXX244	60	MXX260	76	MXX276
13	KYY513	29	MXX229	45	MXX245	61	MXX261		
14	KYY514	30	MXX230	46	MXX246	62	MXX262		
15	KYY515	31	MXX231	47	MXX247	63	MXX263		
16	KYY516	32	MXX232	48	MXX248	64	MXX264		

By the time RM 1 entered trial service in February 1956, several important changes had been made to its specification, including the installation of a saloon heating and ventilating system which led to the substitution of fixed glass for opening windows at the front. The indicator displays were also brought closer to earlier standards with the provision of a full display, although the front intermediate point blind had to be smaller to give space for the heater intake grille. It is seen at Crystal Palace Parade with the buildings of the old High Level station in the background, soon after entering experimental service from Cricklewood garage. Lens of Sutton

ROUTEMASTER

The Routemaster was the last new model to be inspired by the London Passenger Transport Board who authorised design work to start in 1947. This was carried out jointly by London Transport, AEC Ltd and Park Royal Vehicles Ltd and the prototype (RM 1) was completed in 1954. The Routemaster is a fully chassisless vehicle in which all running units (engine, gearbox, axles, suspension and brakes) are attached to an aluminium alloy body built as a rigid box. It was built to the maximum box dimensions permitted at the time: 27 ft long and 8ft wide; but the radiator and fan were installed under the floor to enable the front bulkhead to be moved forward. This, combined with a more upright front to the body, enabled the capacity to be increased to a total of sixty-four (36 up; 28 down). Other new features in the RM were: independent front suspension; coil springs; power hydraulic brakes; and a hydraulically operated direct acting epicyclic gearbox. The 9.6 litre A204 engine was the same as the RT.

After seven months trial service, RM 1 was withdrawn for modifications to the front end, which resulted in a radiator grille being added as an untidy projection, spoiling the proportions of the design. RM 1 is seen in its modified state at Golders Green, accompanied by RTL 1559, also a product of 1954. G.H.F. Atkins

The second prototype, RM 2, had the new AEC AV470 7.7 litre 112 bhp engine, a fully automatic gearbox and power steering but was otherwise similar. In furtherance of the Executive's policy of having an alternative source of supply, two further proto-types were built with Leyland running units incorporating the O600 9.8 litre engine but with the same Self Changing Gears epicyclic gearbox as RMs 1 and 2. RML 3 had a Weymann body of basically the same design but with detailed differences which became the basis for the production run. CRL 4 was a fifty-seven seat coach body built by Eastern Coach Works of Lowestoft. Both RML 3 and CRL 4 had a conventional radiator and a revised style of grille which projected from the bonnet, increasing the length of the bus to 27ft 4ins. The modified radiator and grille had been installed on RMs 1 and 2 after early running trials and was possible because the regulations were altered in 1956 to allow double-deck buses to be built to a length of thirty feet. During this rebuilding, power steering was fitted to RM 1 and its A204 engine was replaced by the new 9.6 litre AV590 (at first called AV600). The AV590 engine was also fitted to RM 2, in 1955.

RM 1 was shown at the Commercial Motor Show in September 1954. At this stage it had very restricted indicator displays as part of the drive towards weight saving. Only one small box was provided at the front and rear and a destination display on the side over the platform. It did not enter passenger service until 8th February 1956, at Cricklewood garage on route 2, by which time a full set of displays had been fitted and saloon heaters installed, the first on a standard London bus. In the meantime it undertook extensive testing, including fuel consumption tests in April and May 1955 at the MIRA proving ground at Nuneaton and rigorous endurance and safety trials for six weeks in June and July 1955 at the Ministry of Supply's Fighting Vehicle Proving Ground at Chobham. RM 2 joined RM 1 on these tests but did not enter service until 20th May 1957 when it appeared in Lincoln green and cream Country Bus livery at Reigate on route 406 but spent only eleven weeks there before being returned to Chiswick on 8th August. It was then repainted red and went to Turnham Green for service on route 91 from 18th September. In February 1958 RM 2 was withdrawn and fitted with air springs at the rear and the new D182 electro-pneumatic gearbox. CRL 4 was allocated to Romford for route 721, where it started work on 9th October 1957. Before going into service its longitudinal seats at the rear of the lower deck were replaced by four angled single seats, reducing the capacity to fifty-five. RML 3 entered service on 22nd January 1958 at Willesden on route 8. RM 1 was relegated to training duties in December 1959, RM 2 and RML 3 in November 1959. CRL 4 undertook a tour of various Green Line routes and was still in service at the end of 1962.

When it finished its trials at Chobham, RM 2 was painted in green Country Bus livery and was fitted with the same type of modified grille as RM 1. It is seen here being inspected before entering service when it had the original version of the new grille which lacked a vertical bar at the centre. B.A. Jenkins

RM 2 first saw service briefly as a green Country Bus on route 406 but was repainted red in August 1957 and spent its main spell of trial running from Turnham Green garage on route 91 on which it is seen at the Wandsworth Bridge terminus in Breer Street, Fulham, in March 1959. The ungainly projecting radiator grille replaced the original neater arrangement in the summer of 1955, when the larger AV590 9.6 litre engine was substituted for the AV470 7.68 litre unit. D.W.K. Jones

RML 3 was the only bus Routemaster to have Leyland running units and the only one of the type of have a Weymann body structure. Apart from the untidy looking bonnet and radiator grille, RML 3 established the appearance which was to be standard on the production vehicles, with a neater finish for the front dome and a better looking heater intake. It spent its spectacularly short operating life on route 8 or on Sundays, as here at Willesden, 8B. A.B. Cross

The only other Routemaster to have Leyland running units was the prototype Green Line version CRL 4, which was also the only one to have an Eastern Coach Works body. Its Leyland pedigree is evident only in the flattened profile of its hub cap in this photograph taken at Windsor when it was in experimental service from Epping garage on route 718. R. Butler

The overall appearance of the back of CRL 4 was the same as the other Routemasters but the inclusion of platform doors made a considerable difference to the lower deck, particularly the three sizes of window imposed by the presence of the emergency exit door. The arrangement of the relief band around the windows gave the whole an assymetrical look. E.J. Smith

An initial order for 850 Routemasters was placed with AEC and Park Royal at the end of 1956 and the production version of the RM first appeared at the Commercial Motor Show in September 1958, when RM 8 was on the Park Royal stand. Its appearance was similar to RML 3 but it had a new design of front nearside wing, bonnet and radiator grille, with built-in registration number plate, which projected in a slight snout. Mechanically, the production batch included the modifications already made to the prototypes, including the electro-pneumatic gearbox and power steering. Various types and combination of electrical and control equipment have been tried, giving rise to the large number of body and chassis codes. Another experiment on RMs 8, 75 and 87–135 was air suspension at the rear, as already tried on RM 2, using four types of suspension.

The production version of the Routemaster began to enter stock in May 1959 and between June and October up to forty-five were operated on a variety of routes to gain experience of the new type. One of the last to be used in this way was RM 96, seen at Hounslow West station in October 1959. Ken Glazier

Like the prototypes, the first 249 production Routemasters did not have opening windows at the front but otherwise set the standard from which all later versions were derived. The first scheduled allocation was made for the Barking Road trolleybus conversion on 11th November 1959. Route 9, on which RM 66 is seen near Poplar garage incorrectly displaying route 23 via blinds, had a long established Sunday extension to Becontree Heath.
Lens of Sutton

Because the delivery of production vehicles was seriously delayed, two sets of units were rigged up with lorry bodies so that road tests could be carried out quickly. They followed buses in service to simulate operational conditions. A third set of units was set aside but not used. These were intended to be RMs 5–7, hence the first completed vehicle being RM 8, but this plan was later dropped.

An experimental batch of thirty-foot long seventy-two seaters was built in the second half of 1961, the majority entering service on trolleybus conversion route 104 from Finchley garage. The first four were initially classified ER but the batch entered service as RML 880–903 (7RM7), following a decision to abandon the distinction between AEC and Leyland vehicles. RML 3 and CRL 4 were renumbered RM 3 and RMC 4 at the same time.

This decision was related to a new contract which had been signed with Leyland Motors for the supply of 406 O.600 engines, to be fitted to running units supplied in the normal way by AEC. The first experimental installation was in RM 632, operating at Hanwell garage from 21st June 1961, further experiments being on RM 870 and RM 1009. The first production batch started at RM 1255 which was one of 119 RMs licensed on 12th December 1962. No separate London Transport type code was applied to this model but AEC marked the difference by allocating the code 2R2RH.

From RM 254 onwards, quarter drop opening windows were added to the front upper deck windows of Routemasters. Seen here in Acton, RM 437 first entered service at Hanwell in November 1960, when route 207A was part of the replacement for trolleybus 607.

When first introduced, the experimental batch of long wheelbase Routemasters was confined to Finchley garage and route 104, on which RML 899 is seen at Barnet Hill. The greater length and the additional short bay inserted in the middle of the body were the only differences from the standard model visible from the nearside. Malcolm E. Papes

In August 1962 the first of a production batch of sixty-eight for the Green Line went into service on route 715. RMC 1453–1520 (6RM6) differed from the prototype in having double headlamps and a combined route number and intermediate point display at the front, as well as the other changes that had been made when the standard model went into production.

The last development of the class before the end of 1962 was the forward-entrance thirty-foot version, RMF 1254 (1/7RM8), which seated sixty-nine passengers. Apart from the move of the entrance and staircase to the front and the consequent changes needed at the rear, the basic structure was identical to the RML. The lower deck emergency door was in the rear offside bay, leaving space inside for a full width bench seat across the back of the saloon. The offside route number was moved forward with the staircase panel. A new style of radiator grille was also carried, incorporating the traditional AEC triangle at the top of the central strip.

Production RMs first entered service in June 1959 at Willesden garage, the first of six garages at which groups of up to eight were tried out before they were used in their intended role of replacing trolleybuses. The first allocations for this purpose were on 11th November 1959, fifty-nine at Poplar and fifteen at West Ham. Following completion of the trolleybus conversion in May 1962, Routemasters were to be used for the replacement of the RT family but their entry into service in this role was delayed until the end of the year by a dispute with the platform staff.

The production coach Routemasters began to enter service in August 1962, RMC 1490, at Harlow, being one of the October licensings. The body specification was much the same as CRL 4, but with the modifications applied to the production model buses. It was given a distinctive appearance by the double headlamps and the use of a narrow single piece indicator for route number and intermediate points. G. Mead

Routemasters started to replace RTs in December 1962, when 179 were licensed. Many, from RM 1255 onwards, were fitted with Leyland engines, including Tottenham's RM 1294, seen in Bloomsbury Street on the one-way system opened the previous year. Michael Rooum

The only public London appearance of RMF 1254 in 1962 was at the Commercial Motor Show, where it was displayed on the Park Royal stand. It was a forward entrance version of the RML with its doorway occupying the whole of the first bay and harmonising well with the rest of the design. It continued most of the existing design features but launched a new, more comely version of the radiator grille. The hopeful dressing of the bus for route 104 at Finchley proved to be a false dawn. London Transport

Chassis units: AEC Routemaster R2RH (AEC engines) 2R2RH (Leyland engines); Leyland units: RML 3 and CRL 4

Engine: AEC A204 9.6 litre 125 bhp, derated to 115 bhp (RM 1 only – replaced by AV590 November 1956); AV470 7.7 litre 112 bhp (RM 2 only – replaced by AV590 May 1955); AV590 9.6 litre 125 bhp, derated to 115bhp (RM 5–631, 633–869, 871–1008, 1010–1254 and RMC 1453–1520); or Leyland O600 9.8 litre 125 bhp derated to 115 bhp (RML 3, CRL 4, RM 632, 870, 1009, 1255–1386).

Transmission: AEC D182 4-speed electro-pneumatic fully automatic with fluid flywheel (5–1520); SCG RV35 Wilson type 4-speed electro-hydraulic fully automatic epicyclic, with fluid flywheel (2, 3, 4: RM 1 – direct acting semi-automatic).

Bodywork: LTE (RM 1, 2); Weymann (RML 3); Eastern Coach Works (CRL 4); Park Royal Vehicles (remainder).

Capacity: H36/28R except: CRL 4 H32/23RD – originally H32/25RD; RML 880–903 H40/32R; RMF1254 H38/31FD; RMC 1453–1520 H32/25RD.

L.T. codes: 1RM1, 2RM2, 3RM3, 4RM4, 5RM5 (5–7, 398, 459), 1/5RM5/1 (8–11, 341), 2/5RM5/2 (12–16), 3/5RM5/3 (17–21), 4/5RM5/4 (22–121, 210–252, 333–339), 5/5RM5/5 (122–209, 340, 464), 6/5RM5/6, (253–332, 342–397, 399–458, 460–463, 465–504), 7/5RM5/7 (505–781, 802–849, 1052–1054, 1174–1253), 8/5RM5/8 (782–801, 850–879, 904–1051, 1155–1173, 1255–1386), 9/5RM5/9 (1071–1154), 10/5RM5/10 (1055–1070), 6RM6 (RMC 1453–1520), 7RM7 (RML 880–903), 1/7RM8 (RMF 1254).

Built: 1954 (RM 1); 1955 (RM 2); 1957 (RML 3, CRL 4); 1959–1962 (remainder)

Number built: 1452 (of 2158 on order)

Number in stock: 1.1.55: 1   31.12.62: 1453 (1359 RM; 69 RMC; 24 RML; 1 RMF)

RM		Date into stock	RM		Date into stock	RM		Date into stock
RM 1	SLT56		36	VLT36	10.8.59	71	VLT71	29.9.59
2	SLT57	10.3.55	37	VLT37	23.7.59	72	VLT72	21.9.59
RML 3	SLT58	1.7.57	38	VLT38	11.9.59	73	VLT73	24.9.59
CRL 4	SLT59	14.6.57	39	VLT39	23.7.59	74	VLT74	22.9.59
RM 5	VLT5	4.6.59	40	VLT40	4.9.59	75	VLT75	7.9.59
6	VLT6	11.5.59	41	VLT41	18.8.59	76	VLT76	21.9.59
7	VLT7	3.6.59	42	VLT42	23.7.59	77	VLT77	21.9.59
8	VLT8	7.3 61	43	VLT43	19.8.59	78	VLT78	23.9.59
9	VLT9	20.5.59	44	VLT44	26.8.59	79	VLT79	2.10.59
10	VLT10	11.8.59	45	VLT45	27.8.59	80	VLT80	29.9.59
11	VLT11	20.5.59	46	VLT46	4.9.59	81	VLT81	21.10.59
12	VLT12	3.6.59	47	VLT47	9.9.59	82	VLT82	29.9.59
13	VLT13	5.6.59	48	VLT48	16.9.59	83	VLT83	29.9.59
14	VLT14	4.6.59	49	VLT49	7.9.59	84	VLT84	30.9.59
15	VLT15	4.6.59	50	VLT50	30.9.59	85	VLT85	29.9.59
16	VLT16	5.6.59	51	VLT51	10.9.59	86	VLT86	22.9.59
17	VLT17	8.6.59	52	VLT52	16.9.59	87	VLT87	20.10.59
18	VLT18	9.6.59	53	VLT53	6.10.59	88	VLT88	13.10.59
19	VLT19	11.6.59	54	VLT54	11.9.59	89	VLT89	2.10.59
20	VLT20	11.6.59	55	VLT55	16.9.59	90	VLT90	13.10.59
21	VLT21	28.9.59	56	VLT56	11.9.59	91	VLT91	20.10.59
22	VLT22	3.7.59	57	VLT57	17.9.59	92	VLT92	13.10.59
23	VLT23	19.6.59	58	VLT58	18.9.59	93	VLT93	13.10.59
24	VLT24	3.6.59	59	VLT59	17.9.59	94	VLT94	24.9.59
25	VLT25	3.7.59	60	VLT60	21.9.59	95	VLT95	23.9.59
26	VLT26	24.6.59	61	VLT61	18.9.59	96	VLT96	1.10.59
27	VLT27	29.6.59	62	VLT62	24.9.59	97	VLT97	14.10.59
28	VLT28	3.7.59	63	VLT63	6.10.59	98	VLT98	14.10.59
29	VLT29	8.7.59	64	VLT64	4.11.59	99	VLT99	8.10.59
30	VLT30	16.7.59	65	VLT65	14.10.59	100	VLT100	15.10.59
31	VLT31	16.7.59	66	VLT66	6.10.59	101	VLT101	7.10.59
32	VLT32	8.7.59	67	VLT67	22.10.59	102	VLT102	14.10.59
33	VLT33	9.7.59	68	VLT68	25.9.59	103	VLT103	14.10.59
34	VLT34	17.7.59	69	VLT69	14.10.59	104	VLT104	22.10.59
35	VLT35	23.7.59	70	VLT70	25.9.59	105	VLT105	13.10.59

RML 3 and CRL 4 renumbered RM 3 and RMC 4 in 1961

RM		Date into stock	RM		Date into stock	RM		Date into stock
106	VLT106	15.10.59	176	VLT176	16.12.59	246	VLT246	22.2.60
107	VLT107	13.10.59	177	VLT177	21.12.59	247	VLT247	22.2.60
108	VLT108	22.10.59	178	VLT178	22.12.59	248	VLT248	1.4.60
109	VLT109	20.10.59	179	VLT179	22.12.59	249	VLT249	25.2.60
110	VLT110	23.10.59	180	VLT180	22.12.59	250	VLT250	25.2.60
111	VLT111	13.10.59	181	VLT181	22.12.59	251	VLT251	2.3.60
112	VLT112	20.10.59	182	VLT182	22.12.59	252	VLT252	29.2.60
113	VLT113	19.10.59	183	VLT183	29.12.59	253	VLT253	25.2.60
114	VLT114	16.10.59	184	VLT184	30.12.59	254	VLT254	29.2.60
115	VLT115	22.10.59	185	VLT185	23.12.59	255	VLT255	2.3.60
116	VLT116	22.10.59	186	VLT186	24.12.59	256	VLT256	2.3.60
117	VLT117	26.10.59	187	VLT187	30.12.59	257	VLT257	17.3.60
118	VLT118	12.11.59	188	VLT188	30.12.59	258	VLT258	3.3.60
119	VLT119	4.11.59	189	VLT189	1.1.60	259	VLT259	4.3.60
120	VLT120	4.11.59	190	VLT190	1.1.60	260	VLT260	4.3.60
121	VLT121	4.11.59	191	VLT191	4.1.60	261	VLT261	7.3.60
122	VLT122	4.11.59	192	VLT192	1.1.60	262	VLT262	4.4.60
123	VLT123	4.11.59	193	VLT193	5.1.60	263	VLT263	8.3.60
124	VLT124	11.11.59	194	VLT194	4.1.60	264	VLT264	8.3.60
125	VLT125	4.11.59	195	VLT195	4.1.60	265	VLT265	11.3.60
126	VLT126	10.11.59	196	VLT196	4.1.60	266	VLT266	15.3.60
127	VLT127	10.11.59	197	VLT197	11.1.60	267	VLT267	15.3.60
128	VLT128	16.11.59	198	VLT198	11.1.60	268	VLT268	18.3.60
129	VLT129	11.11.59	199	VLT199	11.1.60	269	VLT269	4.4.60
130	VLT130	6.11.59	200	VLT200	11.1.60	270	VLT270	16.3.60
131	VLT131	9.11.59	201	VLT201	11.1.60	271	VLT271	15.3.60
132	VLT132	11.11.59	202	VLT202	6.1.60	272	VLT272	16.3.60
133	VLT133	10.11.59	203	VLT203	11.1.60	273	VLT273	17.3.60
134	VLT134	11.11.59	204	VLT204	11.1.60	274	VLT274	23.3.60
135	VLT135	10.11.59	205	VLT205	13.1.60	275	VLT275	23.3.60
136	VLT136	11.11.59	206	VLT206	13.1.60	276	VLT276	21.3.60
137	VLT137	6.11.59	207	VLT207	14.1.60	277	VLT277	24.3.60
138	VLT138	11.11.59	208	VLT208	13.1.60	278	VLT278	21.3.60
139	VLT139	11.11.59	209	VLT209	21.1.60	279	VLT279	23.3.60
140	VLT140	12.11.59	210	VLT210	22.1.60	280	VLT280	23.3.60
141	VLT141	12.11.59	211	VLT211	19.1.60	281	VLT281	1.4.60
142	VLT142	16.11.59	212	VLT212	27.1.60	282	VLT282	1.4.60
143	VLT143	17.11.59	213	VLT213	26.1.60	283	VLT283	29.3.60
144	VLT144	25.11.59	214	VLT214	26.1.60	284	VLT284	29.3.60
145	VLT145	18.11.59	215	VLT215	10.2.60	285	VLT285	25.3.60
146	VLT146	16.11.59	216	VLT216	3.2.60	286	VLT286	6.4.60
147	VLT147	20.11.59	217	VLT217	17.2.60	287	VLT287	30.3.60
148	VLT148	19.11.59	218	VLT218	1.2.60	288	VLT288	5.4.60
149	VLT149	20.11.59	219	VLT219	2.2.60	289	VLT289	1.4.60
150	VLT150	19.11.59	220	VLT220	17.2.60	290	VLT290	1.4.60
151	VLT151	20.11.59	221	VLT221	22.2.60	291	VLT291	5.4.60
152	VLT152	20.11.59	222	VLT222	9.2.60	292	VLT292	5.4.60
153	VLT153	26.11.59	223	VLT223	4.2.60	293	VLT293	4.4.60
154	VLT154	26.11.59	224	VLT224	4.2.60	294	VLT294	19.4.60
155	VLT155	2.12.59	225	VLT225	4.2.60	295	VLT295	4.4.60
156	VLT156	27.11.59	226	VLT226	10.2.60	296	VLT296	5.4.60
157	VLT157	25.11.59	227	VLT227	9.2.60	297	VLT297	22.4.60
158	VLT158	27.11.59	228	VLT228	10.2.60	298	VLT298	5.4.60
159	VLT159	30.11.59	229	VLT229	12.2.60	299	VLT299	6.4.60
160	VLT160	2.12.59	230	VLT230	12.2.60	300	VLT300	6.4.60
161	VLT161	30.11.59	231	VLT231	11.2.60	301	WLT301	7.4.60
162	VLT162	2.12.59	232	VLT232	12.2.60	302	WLT302	11.4.60
163	VLT163	2.12.59	233	VLT233	15.2.60	303	WLT303	8.4.60
164	VLT164	9.12.59	234	VLT234	17.2.60	304	WLT304	8.4.60
165	VLT165	3.12.59	235	VLT235	24.2.60	305	WLT305	13.4.60
166	VLT166	3.12.59	236	VLT236	15.2.60	306	WLT306	11.4.60
167	VLT167	7.12.59	237	VLT237	18.2.60	307	WLT307	21.4.60
168	VLT168	11.12.59	238	VLT238	23.2.60	308	WLT308	22.4.60
169	VLT169	8.12.59	239	VLT239	17.2.60	309	WLT309	19.4.60
170	VLT170	16.12.59	240	VLT240	22.2.60	310	WLT310	19.4.60
171	VLT171	9.12.59	241	VLT241	17.2.60	311	WLT311	19.4.60
172	VLT172	11.12.59	242	VLT242	1.3.60	312	WLT312	20.4.60
173	VLT173	11.12.59	243	VLT243	18.2.60	313	WLT313	21.4.60
174	VLT174	10.12.59	244	VLT244	22.2.60	314	WLT314	26.4.60
175	VLT175	17.12.59	245	VLT245	25.2.60	315	WLT315	22.4.60

RM		Date into stock	RM		Date into stock	RM		Date into stock
316	WLT316	22.4.60	386	WLT386	23.6.60	456	WLT456	8.9.60
317	WLT317	25.4.60	387	WLT387	28.6.60	457	WLT457	7.9.60
318	WLT318	25.4.60	388	WLT388	29.6.60	458	WLT458	2.9.60
319	WLT319	27.4.60	389	WLT389	30.6.60	459	WLT459	1.9.60
320	WLT320	25.4.60	390	WLT390	28.6.60	460	WLT460	16.9.60
321	WLT321	26.4.60	391	WLT391	29.6.60	461	WLT461	6.9.60
322	WLT322	26.4.60	392	WLT392	1.7.60	462	WLT462	8.9.60
323	WLT323	27.4.60	393	WLT393	8.7.60	463	WLT463	6.9.60
324	WLT324	29.4.60	394	WLT394	30.6.60	464	WLT464	2.9.60
325	WLT325	29.4.60	395	WLT395	4.7.60	465	WLT465	8.9.60
326	WLT326	3.5.60	396	WLT396	4.7.60	466	WLT466	12.9.60
327	WLT327	4.5.60	397	WLT397	4.7.60	467	WLT467	12.9.60
328	WLT328	3.5.60	398	WLT398	4.7.60	468	WLT468	13.9.60
329	WLT329	5.5.60	399	WLT399	4.7.60	469	WLT469	14.9.60
330	WLT330	4.5.60	400	WLT400	7.7.60	470	WLT470	14.9.60
331	WLT331	4.5.60	401	WLT401	7.7.60	471	WLT471	5.9.60
332	WLT332	10.5.60	402	WLT402	6.7.60	472	WLT472	16.9.60
333	WLT333	10.5.60	403	WLT403	11.7.60	473	WLT473	9.9.60
334	WLT334	12.5.60	404	WLT404	8.7.60	474	WLT474	14.9.60
335	WLT335	10.5.60	405	WLT405	11.7.60	475	WLT475	13.9.60
336	WLT336	12.5.60	406	WLT406	11.7.60	476	WLT476	13.9.60
337	WLT337	13.5.60	407	WLT407	13.7.60	477	WLT477	15.9.60
338	WLT338	17.5.60	408	WLT408	18.7.60	478	WLT478	13.9.60
339	WLT339	16.5.60	409	WLT409	18.7.60	479	WLT479	16.9.60
340	WLT340	16.5.60	410	WLT410	19.7.60	480	WLT480	16.9.60
341	WLT341	23.5.60	411	WLT411	20.7.60	481	WLT481	10.10.60
342	WLT342	17.5.60	412	WLT412	25.7.60	482	WLT482	19.9.60
343	WLT343	16.5.60	413	WLT413	18.7.60	483	WLT483	16.9.60
344	WLT344	18.5.60	414	WLT414	19.7.60	484	WLT484	19.9.60
345	WLT345	18.5.60	415	WLT415	20.7.60	485	WLT485	19.9.60
346	WLT346	18.5.60	416	WLT416	19.7.60	486	WLT486	22.9.60
347	WLT347	1.6.60	417	WLT417	22.7.60	487	WLT487	19.9.60
348	WLT348	20.5.60	418	WLT418	20.7.60	488	WLT488	22.9.60
349	WLT349	26.5.60	419	WLT419	25.7.60	489	WLT489	22.9.60
350	WLT350	20.5.60	420	WLT420	22.7.60	490	WLT490	20.9.60
351	WLT351	20.5.60	421	WLT421	22.7.60	491	WLT491	20.9.60
352	WLT352	24.5.60	422	WLT422	4.11.60	492	WLT492	28.9.60
353	WLT353	23.5.60	423	WLT423	4.8.60	493	WLT493	6.10.60
354	WLT354	24.5.60	424	WLT424	26.7.60	494	WLT494	19.10.60
355	WLT355	30.5.60	425	WLT425	28.7.60	495	WLT495	22.9.60
356	WLT356	25.5.60	426	WLT426	26.7.60	496	WLT496	28.9.60
357	WLT357	26.5.60	427	WLT427	26.7.60	497	WLT497	30.9.60
358	WLT358	3.6.60	428	WLT428	28.7.60	498	WLT498	27.9.60
359	WLT359	30.5.60	429	WLT429	27.7.60	499	WLT499	27.9.60
360	WLT360	31.5.60	430	WLT430	28.7.60	500	WLT500	3.10.60
361	WLT361	30.5.60	431	WLT431	1.8.60	501	WLT501	28.9.60
362	WLT362	30.5.60	432	WLT432	3.8.60	502	WLT502	21.10.60
363	WLT363	2.6.60	433	WLT433	1.8.60	503	WLT503	30.9.60
364	WLT364	24.6.60	434	WLT434	3.8.60	504	WLT504	30.9.60
365	WLT365	2.6.60	435	WLT435	11.8.60	505	WLT505	4.10.60
366	WLT366	7.6.60	436	WLT436	3.8.60	506	WLT506	3.10.60
367	WLT367	8.6.60	437	WLT437	4.8.60	507	WLT507	9.11.60
368	WLT368	9.6.60	438	WLT438	5.8.60	508	WLT508	20.10.60
369	WLT369	10.6.60	439	WLT439	5.8.60	509	WLT509	28.9.60
370	WLT370	13.6.60	440	WLT440	5.8.60	510	WLT510	4.10.60
371	WLT371	14.6.60	441	WLT441	5.8.60	511	WLT511	7.10.60
372	WLT372	13.6.60	442	WLT442	5.8.60	512	WLT512	4.10.60
373	WLT373	17.6.60	443	WLT443	24.8.60	513	WLT513	1.11.60
374	WLT374	16.6. 60	444	WLT444	23.8.60	514	WLT514	12.10.60
375	WLT375	20.7.60	445	WLT445	22.8.60	515	WLT515	11.10.60
376	WLT376	16.6. 60	446	WLT446	22.8.60	516	WLT516	10.10.60
377	WLT377	15.6.60	447	WLT447	22.8.60	517	WLT517	10.10.60
378	WLT378	20.6.60	448	WLT448	5.9.60	518	WLT518	12.10.60
379	WLT379	17.6.60	449	WLT449	31.8.60	519	WLT519	7.10.60
380	WLT380	16.6. 60	450	WLT450	29.8.60	520	WLT520	10.10.60
381	WLT381	27.6.60	451	WLT451	5.9.60	521	WLT521	11.10.60
382	WLT382	23.6.60	452	WLT452	2.9.60	522	WLT522	10.10.60
383	WLT383	22.6.60	453	WLT453	28.9.60	523	WLT523	14.10.60
384	WLT384	22.6.60	454	WLT454	29.8.60	524	WLT524	12.10.60
385	WLT385	23.6.60	455	WLT455	7.9.60	525	WLT525	14.10.60

RM		Date into stock	RM		Date into stock	RM		Date into stock
526	WLT526	14.10.60	596	WLT596	2.12.60	666	WLT666	25.1.61
527	WLT527	17.10.60	597	WLT597	7.12.60	667	WLT667	25.1.61
528	WLT528	17.10.60	598	WLT598	15.12.60	668	WLT668	3.2.61
529	WLT529	17.10.60	599	WLT599	1.12.60	669	WLT669	27.1.61
530	WLT530	18.10.60	600	WLT600	4.1.61	670	WLT670	27.1.61
531	WLT531	18.10.60	601	WLT601	7.12.60	671	WLT671	30.1.61
532	WLT532	20.10.60	602	WLT602	16.12.60	672	WLT672	31.1.61
533	WLT533	26.10.60	603	WLT603	12.12.60	673	WLT673	1.2.61
534	WLT534	21.10.60	604	WLT604	7.12.60	674	WLT674	30.1.61
535	WLT535	26.10.60	605	WLT605	7.12.60	675	WLT675	31.1.61
536	WLT536	26.10.60	606	WLT606	9.12.60	676	WLT676	31.1.61
537	WLT537	27.10.60	607	WLT607	14.12.60	677	WLT677	6.2.61
538	WLT538	26.10.60	608	WLT608	13.12.60	678	WLT678	6.2.61
539	WLT539	27.10.60	609	WLT609	9.12.60	679	WLT679	3.2.61
540	WLT540	28.10.60	610	WLT610	7.12.60	680	WLT680	3.2.61
541	WLT541	27.10.60	611	WLT611	14.12.60	681	WLT681	8.2.61
542	WLT542	27.10.60	612	WLT612	16.12.60	682	WLT682	6.2.61
543	WLT543	31.10.60	613	WLT613	16.12.60	683	WLT683	28.2.61
544	WLT544	31.10.60	614	WLT614	15.12.60	684	WLT684	10.2.61
545	WLT545	2.11.60	615	WLT615	16.12.60	685	WLT685	9.2.61
546	WLT546	31.10.60	616	WLT616	16.12.60	686	WLT686	9.2.61
547	WLT547	31.10.60	617	WLT617	16.1.61	687	WLT687	10.2.61
548	WLT548	2.11.60	618	WLT618	23.12.60	688	WLT688	10.2.61
549	WLT549	2.11.60	619	WLT619	23.12.60	689	WLT689	17.2.61
550	WLT550	4.11.60	620	WLT620	20.12.60	690	WLT690	16.2.61
551	WLT551	4.11.60	621	WLT621	29.12.60	691	WLT691	14.2.61
552	WLT552	4.11.60	622	WLT622	21.12.60	692	WLT692	17.2.61
553	WLT553	4.11.60	623	WLT623	23.12.60	693	WLT693	17.2.61
554	WLT554	4.11.60	624	WLT624	9.1.61	694	WLT694	15.2.61
555	WLT555	8.11.60	625	WLT625	2.1.61	695	WLT695	16.2.61
556	WLT556	8.11.60	626	WLT626	30.12.60	696	WLT696	24.2.61
557	WLT557	8.11.60	627	WLT627	21.12.60	697	WLT697	17.2.61
558	WLT558	17.11.60	628	WLT628	29.12.60	698	WLT698	16.2.61
559	WLT559	9.11.60	629	WLT629	28.12.60	699	WLT699	21.2.61
560	WLT560	11.11.60	630	WLT630	28.12.60	700	WLT700	20.2.61
561	WLT561	9.11.60	631	WLT631	30.12.60	701	WLT701	23.2.61
562	WLT562	21.11.60	632	WLT632	6.1.61	702	WLT702	20.2.61
563	WLT563	22.11.60	633	WLT633	3.1.61	703	WLT703	24.2.61
564	WLT564	11.11.60	634	WLT634	3.1.61	704	WLT704	23.2.61
565	WLT565	11.11.60	635	WLT635	3.1.61	705	WLT705	1.3.61
566	WLT566	15.11.60	636	WLT636	11.1.61	706	WLT706	23.2.61
567	WLT567	15.11.60	637	WLT637	10.1.61	707	WLT707	28.2.61
568	WLT568	15.11.60	638	WLT638	5.1.61	708	WLT708	24.2.61
569	WLT569	21.11.60	639	WLT639	12.1.61	709	WLT709	24.2.61
570	WLT570	18.11.60	640	WLT640	9.1.61	710	WLT710	23.2.61
571	WLT571	16.11.60	641	WLT641	9.1.61	711	WLT711	28.2.61
572	WLT572	24.11.60	642	WLT642	12.1.61	712	WLT712	2.3.61
573	WLT573	2.12.60	643	WLT643	6.1.61	713	WLT713	2.3.61
574	WLT574	17.11.60	644	WLT644	12.1.61	714	WLT714	9.3.61
575	WLT575	21.11.60	645	WLT645	12.1.61	715	WLT715	6.3.61
576	WLT576	29.11.60	646	WLT646	13.1.61	716	WLT716	3.3.61
577	WLT577	23.11.60	647	WLT647	19.1.61	717	WLT717	6.3.61
578	WLT578	18.11.60	648	WLT648	13.1.61	718	WLT718	1.3.61
579	WLT579	1.12.60	649	WLT649	13.1.61	719	WLT719	7.3.61
580	WLT580	12.12.60	650	WLT650	18.1.61	720	WLT720	6.3.61
581	WLT581	24.11.60	651	WLT651	16.1.61	721	WLT721	6.3.61
582	WLT582	24.11.60	652	WLT652	17.1.61	722	WLT722	6.3.61
583	WLT583	29.11.60	653	WLT653	6.2.61	723	WLT723	7.3.61
584	WLT584	25.11.60	654	WLT654	19.1.61	724	WLT724	7.3.61
585	WLT585	25.11.60	655	WLT655	20.1.61	725	WLT725	9.3.61
586	WLT586	9.12.60	656	WLT656	20.1.61	726	WLT726	8.3.61
587	WLT587	28.11.60	657	WLT657	20.1.61	727	WLT727	9.3.61
588	WLT588	28.11.60	658	WLT658	23.1.61	728	WLT728	9.3.61
589	WLT589	28.11.60	659	WLT659	23.1.61	729	WLT729	10.3.61
590	WLT590	28.11.60	660	WLT660	24.1.61	730	WLT730	14.3.61
591	WLT591	1.12.60	661	WLT661	23.1.61	731	WLT731	10.3.61
592	WLT592	2.12.60	662	WLT662	26.1.61	732	WLT732	14.3.61
593	WLT593	1.12.60	663	WLT663	26.1.61	733	WLT733	14.3.61
594	WLT594	29.11.60	664	WLT664	12.7.61	734	WLT734	15.3.61
595	WLT595	29.11.60	665	WLT665	27.1.61	735	WLT735	17.3.61

RM		Date into stock	RM		Date into stock	RM		Date into stock
736	WLT736	29.3.61	784	WLT784	25.4.61	832	WLT832	13.6.61
737	WLT737	16.3.61	785	WLT785	26.4.61	833	WLT833	14.6.61
738	WLT738	24.3.61	786	WLT786	28.4.61	834	WLT834	21.6.61
739	WLT739	17.3.61	787	WLT787	27.4.61	835	WLT835	13.6.61
740	WLT740	21.3.61	788	WLT788	28.4.61	836	WLT836	15.6.61
741	WLT741	22.3.61	789	WLT789	12.5.61	837	WLT837	16.6. 61
742	WLT742	21.3.61	790	WLT790	2.5.61	838	WLT838	27.6.61
743	WLT743	22.3.61	791	WLT791	3.5.61	839	WLT839	15.6.61
744	WLT744	23.3.61	792	WLT792	4.5.61	840	WLT840	15.6.61
745	WLT745	24.3.61	793	WLT793	4.5.61	841	WLT841	23.6.61
746	WLT746	24.3.61	794	WLT794	13.5.61	842	WLT842	16.6. 61
747	WLT747	24.3.61	795	WLT795	8.5.61	843	WLT843	21.6.61
748	WLT748	27.3.61	796	WLT796	8.5.61	844	WLT844	16.6. 61
749	WLT749	27.3.61	797	WLT797	10.5.61	845	WLT845	21.6.61
750	WLT750	27.3.61	798	WLT798	12.5.61	846	WLT846	23.6.61
751	WLT751	18.4.61	799	WLT799	12.5.61	847	WLT847	22.6.61
752	WLT752	29.3.61	800	WLT800	12.5.61	848	WLT848	23.6.61
753	WLT753	30.3.61	801	WLT801	15.5.61	849	WLT849	30.6.61
754	WLT754	29.3.61	802	WLT802	17.5.61	850	WLT850	23.6.61
755	WLT755	29.3.61	803	WLT803	17.5.61	851	WLT851	30.6.61
756	WLT756	5.4.61	804	WLT804	19.5.61	852	WLT852	30.6.61
757	WLT757	4.4.61	805	WLT805	25.5.61	853	WLT853	30.6.61
758	WLT758	14.4.61	806	WLT806	19.5.61	854	WLT854	30.6.61
759	WLT759	6.4.61	807	WLT807	19.5.61	855	WLT855	30.6.61
760	WLT760	6.4.61	808	WLT808	24.5.61	856	WLT856	30.6.61
761	WLT761	6.4.61	809	WLT809	24.5.61	857	WLT857	5.7.61
762	WLT762	7.4.61	810	WLT810	26.5.61	858	WLT858	5.7.61
763	WLT763	10.4.61	811	WLT811	25.5.61	859	WLT859	30.6.61
764	WLT764	6.4.61	812	WLT812	26.5.61	860	WLT860	30.6.61
765	WLT765	10.4.61	813	WLT813	26.5.61	861	WLT861	7.7.61
766	WLT766	10.4.61	814	WLT814	1.6.61	862	WLT862	7.7.61
767	WLT767	12.4.61	815	WLT815	29.5.61	863	WLT863	7.7.61
768	WLT768	11.4.61	816	WLT816	31.5.61	864	WLT864	7.7.61
769	WLT769	14.4.61	817	WLT817	2.6.61	865	WLT865	13.7.61
770	WLT770	14.4.61	818	WLT818	31.5.61	866	WLT866	12.7.61
771	WLT771	17.4.61	819	WLT819	1.6.61	867	WLT867	14.7.61
772	WLT772	12.4.61	820	WLT820	1.6.61	868	WLT868	18.7.61
773	WLT773	19.4.61	821	WLT821	2.6.61	869	WLT869	19.7.61
774	WLT774	17.4.61	822	WLT822	2.6.61	870	WLT870	21.7.61
775	WLT775	14.4.61	823	WLT823	2.6.61	871	WLT871	12.7.61
776	WLT776	19.4.61	824	WLT824	5.6.61	872	WLT872	12.7.61
777	WLT777	20.4.61	825	WLT825	16.8.61	873	WLT873	19.7.61
778	WLT778	20.4.61	826	WLT826	13.6.61	874	WLT874	14.7.61
779	WLT779	24.4.61	827	WLT827	13.6.61	875	WLT875	14.7.61
780	WLT780	24.4.61	828	WLT828	13.6.61	876	WLT876	27.7.61
781	WLT781	24.4.61	829	WLT829	9.6.61	877	WLT877	19.7.61
782	WLT782	25.4.61	830	WLT830	14.6.61	878	WLT878	21.7.61
783	WLT783	26.4.61	831	WLT831	9.6.61	879	WLT879	21.7.61

RML		Date into stock	RML		Date into stock	RML		Date into stock
* 880	WLT880	10.7.61	888	WLT888	11.10.61	896	WLT896	22.11.61
* 881	WLT881	1.8.61	889	WLT889	6.10.61	897	WLT897	17.11.61
* 882	WLT882	22.8.61	890	WLT890	19.10.61	898	WLT898	6.12.61
* 883	WLT883	30.8.61	891	WLT891	13.10.61	899	WLT899	6.12.61
884	WLT884	4.9.61	892	WLT892	26.10.61	900	WLT900	22.12.61
885	WLT885	14.9.61	893	WLT893	27.10.61	901	WLT901	18.12.61
886	WLT886	20.9 61	894	WLT894	1.11.61	902	WLT902	5.1.62
887	WLT887	29.9.61	895	WLT895	2.11.61	903	WLT903	8.1.62

RM		Date into stock	RM		Date into stock	RM		Date into stock
904	WLT904	28.7.61	908	WLT908	2.8.61	912	WLT912	8.8.61
905	WLT905	1.8.61	909	WLT909	9.8.61	913	WLT913	8.8.61
906	WLT906	1.8.61	910	WLT910	8.8.61	914	WLT914	8.8.61
907	WLT907	2.8.61	911	WLT911	10.8.61	915	WLT915	10.8.61

* RML 880–883 delivered as ER 880–883.

RM		Date into stock	RM		Date into stock	RM		Date into stock
916	WLT916	10.8.61	986	WLT986	12.10.61	1056	56CLT	18.12.61
917	WLT917	11.8.61	987	WLT987	16.10.61	1057	57CLT	18.12.61
918	WLT918	15.8.61	988	WLT988	16.10.61	1058	58CLT	15.12.61
919	WLT919	15.8.61	989	WLT989	16.10.61	1059	59CLT	18.12.61
920	WLT920	16.8.61	990	WLT990	16.10.61	1060	60CLT	18.12.61
921	WLT921	16.8.61	991	WLT991	19.10.61	1061	61CLT	18.12.61
922	WLT922	22.8.61	992	WLT992	16.11.61	1062	62CLT	20.12.61
923	WLT923	24.8.61	993	WLT993	19.10.61	1063	63CLT	18.12.61
924	WLT924	24.8.61	994	WLT994	24.10.61	1064	64CLT	22.12.61
925	WLT925	25.8.61	995	WLT995	20.10.61	1065	65CLT	20.12.61
926	WLT926	31.8.61	996	WLT996	24.10.61	1066	66CLT	20.12.61
927	WLT927	1.9.61	997	WLT997	24.10.61	1067	67CLT	21.12.61
928	WLT928	30.8.61	998	WLT998	24.10.61	1068	68CLT	22.12.61
929	WLT929	1.9.61	999	WLT999	1.11.61	1069	69CLT	20.12.61
930	WLT930	1.9.61	1000	100BXL	23.10.61	1070	70CLT	22.12.61
931	WLT931	7.9.61	1001	1CLT	27.10.61	1071	71CLT	22.12.61
932	WLT932	1.9.61	1002	2CLT	1.11.61	1072	72CLT	1.1.62
933	WLT933	29.8.61	1003	3CLT	1.11.61	1073	73CLT	22.12.61
934	WLT934	29.8.61	1004	4CLT	27.10.61	1074	74CLT	22.12.61
935	WLT935	25.8.61	1005	5CLT	2.11.61	1075	75CLT	3.1.62
936	WLT936	15.9.61	1006	6CLT	3.11.61	1076	76CLT	1.1.62
937	WLT937	4.9.61	1007	7CLT	3.11.61	1077	77CLT	3.1.62
938	WLT938	5.9.61	1008	8CLT	3.11.61	1078	78CLT	1.1.62
939	WLT939	15.9.61	1009	9CLT	3.11.61	1079	79CLT	1.1.62
940	WLT940	18.9.61	1010	10CLT	13.11.61	1080	80CLT	3.1.62
941	WLT941	19.9.61	1011	11CLT	10.11.61	1081	81CLT	19.1.62
942	WLT942	15.9.61	1012	12CLT	10.11.61	1082	82CLT	8.1.62
943	WLT943	19.9.61	1013	13CLT	9.11.61	1083	83CLT	11.1.62
944	WLT944	18.9.61	1014	14CLT	15.11.61	1084	84CLT	8.1.62
945	WLT945	18.9.61	1015	15CLT	15.11.61	1085	85CLT	10.1.62
946	WLT946	8.9.61	1016	16CLT	17.11.61	1086	86CLT	11.1.62
947	WLT947	15.9.61	1017	17CLT	17.11.61	1087	87CLT	11.1.62
948	WLT948	14.9.61	1018	18CLT	29.11.61	1088	88CLT	9.1.62
949	WLT949	14.9.61	1019	19CLT	24.11.61	1089	89CLT	11.1.62
950	WLT950	14.9.61	1020	20CLT	22.11.61	1090	90CLT	15.1.62
951	WLT951	12.9.61	1021	21CLT	22.11.61	1091	91CLT	17.1.62
952	WLT952	15.9.61	1022	22CLT	22.11.61	1092	92CLT	17.1.62
953	WLT953	14.9.61	1023	23CLT	22.11.61	1093	93CLT	17.1.62
954	WLT954	14.9.61	1024	24CLT	29.11.61	1094	94CLT	15.1.62
955	WLT955	20.9.61	1025	25CLT	24.11.61	1095	95CLT	19.1.62
956	WLT956	22.9.61	1026	26CLT	24.11.61	1096	96CLT	17.1.62
957	WLT957	19.9.61	1027	27CLT	24.11.61	1097	97CLT	19.1.62
958	WLT958	22.9.61	1028	28CLT	29.11.61	1098	98CLT	24.1.62
959	WLT959	21.9.61	1029	29CLT	1.12.61	1099	99CLT	19.1.62
960	WLT960	22.9.61	1030	30CLT	29.11.61	1100	100CLT	22.1.62
961	WLT961	21.9.61	1031	31CLT	17.5.62	1101	101CLT	21.2.62
962	WLT962	21.9.61	1032	32CLT	13.12.61	1102	102CLT	19.1.62
963	WLT963	22.9.61	1033	33CLT	29.11.61	1103	103CLT	24.1.62
964	WLT964	27.9.61	1034	34CLT	1.12.61	1104	104CLT	24.1.62
965	WLT965	11.10.61	1035	35CLT	1.12.61	1105	105CLT	25.1.62
966	WLT966	26.9.61	1036	36CLT	30.11.61	1106	106CLT	25.1.62
967	WLT967	26.9.61	1037	37CLT	6.12.61	1107	107CLT	26.1.62
968	WLT968	29.9.61	1038	38CLT	5.12.61	1108	108CLT	26.1.62
969	WLT969	29.9.61	1039	39CLT	20.12.61	1109	109CLT	31.1.62
970	WLT970	28.9.61	1040	40CLT	6.12.61	1110	110CLT	29.1.62
971	WLT971	29.9.61	1041	41CLT	6.12.61	1111	111CLT	29.1.62
972	WLT972	2.10.61	1042	42CLT	7.12.61	1112	112CLT	30.1.62
973	WLT973	29.9.61	1043	43CLT	8.12.61	1113	113CLT	31.1.62
974	WLT974	2.10.61	1044	44CLT	8.12.61	1114	114CLT	31.1.62
975	WLT975	6.10.61	1045	45CLT	8.12.61	1115	115CLT	31.1.62
976	WLT976	4.10.61	1046	46CLT	11.12.61	1116	116CLT	1.2.62
977	WLT977	4.10.61	1047	47CLT	11.12.61	1117	117CLT	2.2.62
978	WLT978	4.10.61	1048	48CLT	11.12.61	1118	118CLT	7.2.62
979	WLT979	11.10.61	1049	49CLT	13.12.61	1119	119CLT	2.2.62
980	WLT980	6.10.61	1050	50CLT	11.12.61	1120	120CLT	2.2.62
981	WLT981	6.10.61	1051	51CLT	21.12.61	1121	121CLT	5.2.62
982	WLT982	11.10.61	1052	52CLT	13.12.61	1122	122CLT	7.2.62
983	WLT983	13.10.61	1053	53CLT	18.12.61	1123	123CLT	7.2.62
984	WLT984	12.10.61	1054	54CLT	13.12.61	1124	124CLT	7.2.62
985	WLT985	12.10.61	1055	55CLT	14.12.61	1125	125CLT	9.2.62

RM		Date into stock	RM		Date into stock	RM		Date into stock
1126	126CLT	12.2.62	1169	169CLT	19.3.62	1212	212CLT	3.5.62
1127	127CLT	9.2.62	1170	170CLT	22.3.62	1213	213CLT	2.5.62
1128	128CLT	12.2.62	1171	171CLT	22.3.62	1214	214CLT	2.5.62
1129	129CLT	14.2.62	1172	172CLT	22.3.62	1215	215CLT	4.5.62
1130	130CLT	13.2.62	1173	173CLT	23.3.62	1216	216CLT	3.5.62
1131	131CLT	16.2.62	1174	174CLT	30.3.62	1217	217CLT	4.5.62
1132	132CLT	21.2.62	1175	175CLT	23.3.62	1218	218CLT	9.5.62
1133	133CLT	23.2.62	1176	176CLT	26.3.62	1219	219CLT	7.5.62
1134	134CLT	16.2.62	1177	177CLT	28.3.62	1220	220CLT	14.5.62
1135	135CLT	16.2.62	1178	178CLT	29.3.62	1221	221CLT	7.5.62
1136	136CLT	21.2.62	1179	179CLT	28.3.62	1222	222CLT	9.5.62
1137	137CLT	21.2.62	1180	180CLT	11.4.62	1223	223CLT	10.5.62
1138	138CLT	16.2.62	1181	181CLT	30.3.62	1224	224CLT	10.5.62
1139	139CLT	22.2.62	1182	182CLT	29.3.62	1225	225CLT	14.5.62
1140	140CLT	22.2.62	1183	183CLT	30.3.62	1226	226CLT	14.5.62
1141	141CLT	26.2.62	1184	184CLT	30.3.62	1227	227CLT	14.5.62
1142	142CLT	21.2.62	1185	185CLT	4.4.62	1228	228CLT	23.5.62
1143	143CLT	23.2.62	1186	186CLT	2.4.62	1229	229CLT	25.6.62
1144	144CLT	17.5.62	1187	187CLT	4.4.62	1230	230CLT	16.5.62
1145	145CLT	26.2.62	1188	188CLT	4.4.62	1231	231CLT	21.5.62
1146	146CLT	2.3.62	1189	189CLT	4.4.62	1232	232CLT	21.5.62
1147	147CLT	1.3.62	1190	190CLT	5.4.62	1233	233CLT	21.5.62
1148	148CLT	1.3.62	1191	191CLT	5.4.62	1234	234CLT	21.5.62
1149	149CLT	9.3.62	1192	192CLT	6.4.62	1235	235CLT	21.5.62
1150	150CLT	2.3.62	1193	193CLT	9.4.62	1236	236CLT	23.5.62
1151	151CLT	7.3.62	1194	194CLT	9.4.62	1237	237CLT	23.5.62
1152	152CLT	7.3.62	1195	195CLT	11.4.62	1238	238CLT	23.5.62
1153	153CLT	12.3.62	1196	196CLT	11.4.62	1239	239CLT	25.5.62
1154	154CLT	14.3.62	1197	197CLT	11.4.62	1240	240CLT	23.5.62
1155	155CLT	7.3.62	1198	198CLT	13.4.62	1241	241CLT	25.5.62
1156	156CLT	7.3.62	1199	199CLT	25.4.62	1242	242CLT	28.5.62
1157	157CLT	9.3.62	1200	200CLT	16.4.62	1243	243CLT	30.5.62
1158	158CLT	16.3.62	1201	201CLT	25.4.62	1244	244CLT	30.5.62
1159	159CLT	9.3.62	1202	202CLT	13.4.62	1245	245CLT	30.5.62
1160	160CLT	9.3.62	1203	203CLT	18.4.62	1246	246CLT	4.6.62
1161	161CLT	12.3.62	1204	204CLT	24.4.62	1247	247CLT	30.5.62
1162	162CLT	13.3.62	1205	205CLT	26.4.62	1248	248CLT	20.6.62
1163	163CLT	12.3.62	1206	206CLT	24.4.62	1249	249CLT	31.5.62
1164	164CLT	14.3.62	1207	207CLT	24.4.62	1250	250CLT	1.6.62
1165	165CLT	15.3.62	1208	208CLT	30.4.62	1251	251CLT	1.6.62
1166	166CLT	21.3.62	1209	209CLT	27.4.62	1252	252CLT	1.6.62
1167	167CLT	16.3.62	1210	210CLT	27.4.62	1253	253CLT	6.6. 62
1168	168CLT	19.3.62	1211	211CLT	27.4.62			

RMF		Date into stock
1254	254CLT	19.10.62

RM		Date into stock	RM		Date into stock	RM		Date into stock
1255	255CLT	8.6.62	1273	273CLT	25.6.62	1291	291CLT	4.7.62
1256	256CLT	26.4.62	1274	274CLT	22.6.62	1292	292CLT	12.7.62
1257	257CLT	12.6.62	1275	275CLT	27.6.62	1293	293CLT	13.7.62
1258	258CLT	6.6.62	1276	276CLT	28.6.62	1294	294CLT	18.7.62
1259	259CLT	25.6.62	1277	277CLT	25.6.62	1295	295CLT	16.7.62
1260	260CLT	12.6.62	1278	278CLT	25.6.62	1296	296CLT	16.7.62
1261	261CLT	8.6.62	1279	279CLT	25.6.62	1297	297CLT	18.7.62
1262	262CLT	8.6.62	1280	280CLT	28.6.62	1298	298CLT	20.7.62
1263	263CLT	8.6.62	1281	281CLT	4.7.62	1299	299CLT	20.7.62
1264	264CLT	8.6.62	1282	282CLT	28.6.62	1300	300CLT	22.8.62
1265	265CLT	14.6.62	1283	283CLT	4.7.62	1301	301CLT	29.8.62
1266	266CLT	13.6.62	1284	284CLT	4.7.62	1302	302CLT	30.8.62
1267	267CLT	14.6.62	1285	285CLT	4.7.62	1303	303CLT	31.8.62
1268	268CLT	14.6.62	1286	286CLT	11.7.62	1304	304CLT	7.9.62
1269	269CLT	18.6.62	1287	287CLT	6.7.62	1305	305CLT	4.9.62
1270	270CLT	20.6.62	1288	288CLT	6.7.62	1306	306CLT	7.9.62
1271	271CLT	20.6.62	1289	289CLT	6.7.62	1307	307CLT	5.9.62
1272	272CLT	21.6.62	1290	290CLT	11.7.62	1308	308CLT	7.9.62

RM		Date into stock	RM		Date into stock	RM		Date into stock
1309	309CLT	7.9.62	1335	335CLT	31.10.62	1361	361CLT	28.11.62
1310	310CLT	7.9.62	1336	336CLT	26.10.62	1362	362CLT	26.11.62
1311	311CLT	14.9.62	1337	337CLT	2.11.62	1363	363CLT	28.11.62
1312	312CLT	13.9.62	1338	338CLT	2.11.62	1364	364CLT	28.11.62
1313	313CLT	14.9.62	1339	339CLT	31.10.62	1365	365CLT	29.11.62
1314	314CLT	26.9.62	1340	340CLT	2.11.62	1366	366CLT	12.12.62
1315	315CLT	19.9.62	1341	341CLT	12.11.62	1367	367CLT	19.12.62
1316	316CLT	21.9.62	1342	342CLT	7.11.62	1368	368CLT	30.11.62
1317	317CLT	21.9.62	1343	343CLT	14.11.62	1369	369CLT	5.12.62
1318	318CLT	21.9.62	1344	344CLT	1.11.62	1370	370CLT	19.12.62
1319	319CLT	27.9.62	1345	345CLT	9.11.62	1371	371CLT	6.12.62
1320	320CLT	5.10.62	1346	346CLT	9.11.62	1372	372CLT	7.12.62
1321	321CLT	28.9.62	1347	347CLT	12.12.62	1373	373CLT	7.12.62
1322	322CLT	2.10.62	1348	348CLT	14.11.62	1374	374CLT	21.12.62
1323	323CLT	3.10.62	1349	349CLT	14.11.62	1375	375CLT	19.12.62
1324	324CLT	3.10.62	1350	350CLT	14.11.62	1376	376CLT	12.12.62
1325	325CLT	3.10.62	1351	351CLT	14.11.62	1377	377CLT	19.12.62
1326	326CLT	5.10.62	1352	352CLT	21.11.62	1378	378CLT	21.12.62
1327	327CLT	5.10.62	1353	353CLT	19.11.62	1379	379CLT	20.12.62
1328	328CLT	12.10.62	1354	354CLT	21.11.62	1380	380CLT	28.12.62
1329	329CLT	12.10.62	1355	355CLT	28.11.62	1381	381CLT	28.12.62
1330	330CLT	24.10.62	1356	356CLT	19.11.62	1382	382CLT	28.12.62
1331	331CLT	18.10.62	1357	357CLT	22.11.62	1383	383CLT	31.12.62
1332	332CLT	24.10.62	1358	358CLT	28.11.62	1385	385CLT	31.12.62
1333	333CLT	18.10.62	1359	359CLT	22.11.62	1386	386CLT	31.12.62
1334	334CLT	24.10.62	1360	360CLT	21.11.62			

RMC		Date into stock	RMC		Date into stock	RMC		Date into stock
1453	453CLT	28.6.62	1476	476CLT	31.8.62	1499	499CLT	31.10.62
1454	454CLT	18.7.62	1477	477CLT	5.9.62	1500	500CLT	8.11.62
1455	455CLT	18.7.62	1478	478CLT	5.9.62	1501	501CLT	7.11.62
1456	456CLT	18.7.62	1479	479CLT	10.9.62	1502	502CLT	7.11.62
1457	457CLT	18.7.62	1480	480CLT	10.9.62	1503	503CLT	8.11.62
1458	458CLT	18.7.62	1481	481CLT	12.9.62	1504	504CLT	16.11.62
1459	459CLT	18.7.62	1482	482CLT	12.9.62	1505	505CLT	16.11.62
1460	460CLT	18.7.62	1483	483CLT	13.9.62	1506	506CLT	14.11.62
1461	461CLT	18.7.62	1484	484CLT	17.9.62	1507	507CLT	19.12.62
1462	462CLT	19.7.62	1485	485CLT	20.9.62	1508	508CLT	29.11.62
1463	463CLT	19.7.62	1486	486CLT	3.10.62	1509	509CLT	22.11.62
1464	464CLT	20.7.62	1487	487CLT	3.10.62	1510	510CLT	26.11.62
1465	465CLT	26.7.62	1488	488CLT	27.9.62	1511	511CLT	19.12.62
1466	466CLT	20.7.62	1489	489CLT	8.10.62	1512	512CLT	5.12.62
1467	467CLT	3.8.62	1490	490CLT	3.10.62	1513	513CLT	6.12.62
1468	468CLT	3.8.62	1491	491CLT	10.10.62	1514	514CLT	12.12.62
1469	469CLT	3.8.62	1492	492CLT	19.10.62	1515	515CLT	14.12.62
1470	470CLT	15.8.62	1493	493CLT	15.10.62	1516	516CLT	14.12.62
1471	471CLT	15.8.62	1494	494CLT	19.10.62	1517	517CLT	14.12.62
1472	472CLT	15.8.62	1495	495CLT	10.10.62	1518	518CLT	17.12.62
1473	473CLT	27.8.62	1496	496CLT	19.10.62	1519	519CLT	20.12.62
1474	474CLT	29.8.62	1497	497CLT	25.10.62	1520	520CLT	20.12.62
1475	475CLT	29.8.62	1498	498CLT	29.10.62			

The Weymann bodies of the early post-war 14T12s were the company's standard design which was also found in many other parts of the country, the only London touches being the large indicator boxes which, at the front, drooped down to cover the top of the windscreen, and at the back swept up to stand proud of the roof. Their last major area of operation before being withdrawn in November 1958 was at Uxbridge, where they maintained the Cowley Road routes, the only others being at Southall on route 211. T 758 was photographed in July 1957 at Bakers Road, Uxbridge, surrounded by the omnipresent RT. Alan B. Cross

T

The T class was first introduced as a bus by the London General Omnibus Company in 1929 and later as a coach for the Green Line services. London Transport acquired a number of similar vehicles from Independent operators and itself purchased fifty oil engined vehicles for Green Line. Only one vehicle survives from the period before 1938, T 31, one of the original LGOC buses. This is believed to be the first bus to have been purchased for private preservation. As part of its large 1938/39 replacement programme London Transport ordered 266 AEC Regals to replace all pre-1936 Green Line coaches. These employed the new AEC pot cavity 8.8 litre oil engine, which had been inspired by the similar engines supplied by Leyland in the STD class. The bodywork was the first production run of composite bodies built in the shops at Chiswick. The first 150 had thirty seats but the last 116 were to a modified design with thirty-four seats. All were converted to ambulances at the outbreak of war and later many were used by the American Red Cross as 'Clubmobiles' or transports. They returned to Green Line service from 1946 and were replaced by the RF and GS classes between 1951 and 1954.

Seen in its home town of Hemel Hempstead, T 779 was one of thirty AEC Regal IIIs bodied by Mann Egerton in 1948. The styling at the front in particular was much neater and well proportioned than the Weymann vehicles. Alan B. Cross

In 1946 London Transport was allotted fifty crash gearbox AEC Regals with 'provincial' standard Weymann thirty-five seat bodywork, which were intended as a stop-gap until vehicles built to LT's own specification could be acquired. Seating capacity was later reduced to thirty-three and then, on twenty-six vehicles to thirty-two. They were first allocated to Uxbridge, Kingston and Muswell Hill garages and later to Southall and Sidcup. Withdrawal began in 1955 and was completed in 1959, the replacements being RFs made redundant by service cuts and double-decking. In 1948 a further thirty Regals were acquired for service expansion in the Country Bus department. They were Regal Mark IIIs with a mechanical specification comparable to the double-deck RTs but their bodywork was a standard product from Mann Egerton of Norwich. They were originally allocated to Hemel Hempstead and Watford (Leavesden Road) garages and later to Garston, Crawley, Grays, Tring, Hatfield and Amersham. Withdrawal of the 15T13s began in the autumn of 1956 as surplus RFs was used to convert routes to one-man operation. Some of them were used as trainers or staff buses. In September 1956 two were lent to Central Buses for operation at Norbiton and these were joined by another ten in 1957. There were plans to repaint 15T13s red for Central Bus use but these were never put into practice. The last 15T13, which was also the last T, was delicensed at Crawley on 13th August 1962 and at the end of the year only four remained in stock, all in store awaiting disposal.

At the beginning of 1955 the sole survivor of the large fleet of new buses put into service by the LGOC between 1929 and 1932 was T 31. It had not been refurbished by Marshalls in 1949 and its appearance was therefore little changed from the original 1929 design. It had been withdrawn from passenger service in 1953 and these two photographs were taken in Chiswick Works while it was in use as a trainer. It survived long enough to be sold for private preservation. *John Gillham*

Chassis:	AEC Regal 0662 (T 31, 593–768) or Mk III 0962/9621E (T 769–798)
Engine:	AEC A171 6-cylinder 7.7 litre 95 bhp oil (31); A180 6-cyl. 8.8 litre direct injection 100 bhp oil (593–717); A173 7.7 litre direct injection 95 bhp oil (719–768); or A208 6-cylinder 9.6 litre direct injection 125 bhp oil (769–798).
Transmission:	AEC D124 four speed crash (31 and 719–768); D132 direct selection pre-selective with fluid flywheel (593–717); or D140 air operated preselective with fluid flywheel (769–798)
Bodywork:	LGOC (31); LPTB (593–717); Weymann (719–768); Mann Egerton (769–798)
L.T. codes:	1T1 (31); 1/10 or 10T/T10 or 10/1 (593–717); 14T12 (719–768); 15T13 (769–798)
Built:	1929 (31); 1938/39 (493–717); 1946 (719–768); 1948 (769–798)
Number built:	780
Number in stock:	1.1.55: 129 31.12.62: 4

T		Date out of stock	T		Date out of stock	T		Date out of stock
* 31	UU6646	18.10.56	706	EYK341	17.11.56	756	HGF846	5.1.59
593	EYK228	15.7.55	707	EYK342	17.11.56	757	HGF847	8.12.58
607	EYK242	13.10.56	711	EYK346	11.1.55	758	HGF848	14.1.59
613	EYK248	19.12.56	714	EYK349	17.11.56	759	HGF849	8.12.58
617	EYK252	13.3.57	† 716	EYK351	30.4.57	760	HGF850	8.12.58
619	EYK254	13.3.57	717	EYK352	14.3.57	761	HGF851	14.1.59
621	EYK256	13.3.57	719	HGF809	5.1.59	762	HGF852	5.1.59
624	EYK259	13.3.57	720	HGF810	5.1.59	763	HGF853	8.12.58
626	EYK261	3.9.56	721	HGF811	27.2.56	764	HGF854	14.1 59
628	EYK263	6.1.55	722	HGF812	16.8.55	765	HGF855	5.1.59
629	EYK264	13.10.56	723	HGF813	27.2.56	766	HGF856	5.1.59
631	EYK266	13.3.57	724	HGF814	5.1.59	767	HGF857	14.1.59
634	EYK269	8.6.55	725	HGF815	19.3.56	768	HGF858	5.1.59
635	EYK270	4.1.55	726	HGF816	27.2.56	769	HLX439	22.4.58
636	EYK271	23.6.55	727	HGF817	27.2.56	770	HLX440	22.4.58
637	EYK272	4.1.55	728	HGF818	17.8.55	771	HLX441	22.4.58
639	EYK274	13.3.57	729	HGF819	18.8.55	772	HLX442	19.3.56
641	EYK276	13.10.56	730	HGF820	28.2.56	773	HLX443	7.4.60
642	EYK277	14.3.57	731	HGF821	28.2.56	774	HLX444	19.3.56
645	EYK280	16.1.55	732	HGF822	28.2.56	775	HLX445	22.4.58
646	EYK281	16.1.55	733	HGF823	28.2.56	776	HLX446	19.3.56
647	EYK282	13.10.56	734	HGF824	16.8.55	777	HLX447	22.4.56
650	EYK285	24.2.55	735	HGF825	16.8.55	778	HLX448	22.4.58
654	EYK289	4.1.55	736	HGF826	16.8.55	779	HLX449	22.4.58
659	EYK294	23.6.55	737	HGF827	29.2.56	780	HLX450	22.7.58
661	EYK296	6.1.55	738	HGF828	17.8.55	781	HLX451	6.11.58
662	EYK297	6.1.55	739	HGF829	29.2.56	782	HLX452	1.8.59
667	EYK302	6.2.56	740	HGF830	17.8.55	783	HLX453	22.4.58
668	EYK303	13.10.56	741	HGF831	29.2.56	784	HLX454	7.4.60
669	EYK304	14.3.57	742	HGF832	18.8.55	785	HLX455	
671	EYK306	13.10.56	743	HGF833	14.1.59	786	HLX456	7.4.60
673	EYK308	13.10.56	744	HGF834	8.12.58	787	HLX457	
676	EYK311	7.1.57	745	HGF835	25.4.57	788	HLX458	1.8.59
679	EYK314	14.3.57	746	HGF836	14.1.59	789	HLX459	1.8.59
680	EYK315	17.11.56	747	HGF837	14.1.59	790	HLX460	
682	EYK317	13.1.55	748	HGF838	8.12.58	791	HLX461	1.8.59
683	EYK318	11.1.55	749	HGF839	5.1.59	792	HLX462	
684	EYK319	3.2.55	750	HGF840	14.1.59	793	HLX463	22.4.58
688	EYK323	14.3.57	751	HGF841	14.1.59	794	HLX464	7.4.60
692	EYK327	14.3.57	752	HGF842	14.1.59	795	HLX465	1.8.59
693	EYK328	17.11.56	753	HGF843	9.1.59	796	HLX466	7.4.60
697	EYK332	14.3.57	754	HGF844	14.1.59	797	HLX467	1.8.59
705	EYK340	17.11.56	755	HGF845	14.1.59	798	HLX468	1.8.59

* Last 1T1 in stock   † Last 10T10 in stock

C/CR/Q

Examples of three classes of single decker withdrawn from passenger service remained in stock at the beginning of 1955. The Leyland Cub was chosen by London Transport in 1935 as its standard one-man bus and was used to replace the many different types of small bus inherited from Independent operators. The C class Cubs were delivered in 1935 and 1936 and remained in service until replaced by GSs in 1953 and 1954. The CR was a revolutionary new transverse rear engined version of the Cub designed by Leyland and London Transport in 1937. The last of these ran in passenger service in November 1953. Just one example of the once-large Q class dating from 1935 and 1936 remained, converted to a mobile gas unit and renumbered from Q 75 to 1035CD.

C

Chassis:	Leyland Cub KPO3
Engine:	Leyland 6-cylinder 4.4 litre direct injection 65 bhp oil (77–98 – 4.7 litres)
Transmission:	Leyland 4-speed crash
Bodywork:	Short Bros. (4–69); Weymann (77–98)
Capacity:	B20F
Built:	1935 (4–69) or 1936
L.T. codes:	2C2 (4–69); or 1/2C2
Number built:	106
Number in stock:	1.1.55: 21 Last vehicle out of stock: 5.9.55

C		Date out of stock	C		Date out of stock	C		Date out of stock
4	BXD628	24.6.55	50	BXD675	1.7.55	82	CLE110	5.9.55
21	BXD646	30.8.55	53	BXD678	1.7.55	90	CLE118	24.6.55
25	BXD650	8.7.55	59	BXD684	1.7.55	91	CLE119	7.7.55
31	BXD656	12.7.55	69	BXD694	10.5.55	92	CLE120	12.7.55
36	BXD661	1.7.55	77	CLE105	12.7.55	93	CLE121	7.7.55
41	BXD666	14.7.55	78	CLE106	14.7.55	95	CLE123	12.5.55
44	BXD669	13.5.55	81	CLE109	11.5.55	98	CLE126	24.6.55

CR

Chassis:	Leyland REC
Engine:	Leyland 6-cylinder 4.7 litre indirect injection 65 bhp oil
Transmission:	Leyland 4-speed crash (helical third gear)
Bodywork:	LPTB
Capacity:	B20F
L.T. code:	2CR2
Built:	1939
Number built:	49
Number in stock:	1.1.55: 4 Last vehicle out of stock: 6.7.55

CR		Date out of stock	CR		Date out of stock
4	FXT110	10.5.55	10	FXT116	6.7.55
6	FXT112	6.7.55	32	FXT138	25.3.55

Q

Chassis:	AEC 'Q' 0762
Engine:	AEC A170 6-cylinder 7.7 litre 95 bhp oil
Transmission:	AEC 4-speed direct selection preselective with fluid flywheel
Bodywork:	Birmingham Railway Carriage & Wagon Co. Ltd
L.T. code:	4Q4
Capacity:	B35C
Built:	1935/36
Number built:	238
Number in stock:	1.1.55: 1 To service vehicle stock: 28.11.55

75	CGJ180	28.11.55

Converted to Mobile Gas Unit Q1035CD.

Of 238 AEC Qs once owned by London Transport, only Q 75, one of the 102 Country Bus BRCW-bodied 4Q4s, remained in stock at the beginning of 1955. Although looking much as it had when it was a bus, by the time this photograph was taken in Victoria garage 'sidecourt' in 1962, it was a Mobile Gas Unit numbered Q1035CD in the service vehicle fleet. P.J. Relf

One of the original batch of thirty-one TDs allocated to Muswell Hill, TD 28 was photographed at the Staines West station terminus of route 216 in May 1955. These buses had Weymann bodies identical to the 14T12s except for the straight bottom line of the windscreen.
G.H.F. Atkins

The main batch of Leyland Tiger PS1s, classified 1/1TD2, had Mann Egerton bodywork identical to the 15T13s, except that the platform door was omitted and trafficator housings added. TD 105 is at Mill Hill East station, displaying an incorrect blind including the word 'ONLY', which was phased out in the mid-fifties.
P.J. Relf

TD

In 1946, following the delivery of the 14T12s and as part of the same 'stop-gap' programme, London Transport was allotted thirty-one of the new Leyland Tiger PS1 model. They were fitted with 'provincial' standard Weymann bodywork identical to the Ts but with thirty-three seats from the outset. The mechanical specification was the same as for the 4STD3s. The seating capacity was reduced to thirty-two in 1954. All thirty-one were allocated to Muswell Hill garage, where they replaced 14T12s on route 212 between December 1946 and March 1947. They were replaced in turn by RFs in 1952 and transferred to Kingston and Loughton. A repeat order for one hundred similar chassis was placed in 1948 and put into service between October 1948 and October 1949. These had Mann Egerton bodywork identical to that supplied on the 15T13s except that no door was fitted to the passenger entrance. These were used to replace the oldest Ts and single-deck LTs at nine Central Area garages. Withdrawal of the class began in June 1953 when routes 205, 242 and 243 were converted to double-deck operation. Further double-deckings and the gradual decline in service levels reduced the number scheduled for service to forty-three by the end of 1959. The last 1TD1 was taken out of service in March 1958. Withdrawal of the Mann Egertons started soon afterwards, with substantial cuts being made following the 1958 bus strike. The class ran for the last time on 9th October 1962, after which they were replaced on route 240A from Edgware garage by RFs. Fifteen remained in store at the end of the year.

Those TDs remaining in service were fitted with flashing trafficators in 1959/1960.

Chassis:	Leyland Tiger PS1
Engine:	Leyland 6-cylinder 7.4 litre direct injection 100 bhp oil
Transmission:	Leyland 4-speed constant mesh
Bodywork:	Weymann (1–31); or Mann Egerton
Capacity:	B32F (1–31); or B31F
Built:	1946/47 (1–31); 1948/49
L.T. codes:	1TD1 (1–31) or 1/1TD2
Number built:	131
Number in stock:	1.1.55: 131 31.12.62: 15

TD		Date out of stock	TD		Date out of stock	TD		Date out of stock
1	HGF959	3.9.56	45	JXC238	5.1.59	89	JXC282	29.11.62
2	HGF960	20.8.56	46	JXC239	14.1.59	90	JXC283	6.10.62
3	HGF961	7.9.56	47	JXC240	1.8.59	91	JXC284	25.3.60
4	HGF962	7.9.56	48	JXC241	5.1.59	92	JXC285	25.3.60
5	HGF963	7.9.56	49	JXC242	1.8.59	93	JXC286	7.4.60
6	HGF964	20.8.56	50	JXC243	14.1.59	94	JXC287	25.3.60
7	HGF965	3.9.56	51	JXC244	1.8.59	95	JXC288	
8	HGF966	22.4.58	52	JXC245	5.1.59	96	JXC289	25.3.60
9	HGF967.	11.8.58	53	JXC246	5.1.59	97	JXC290	25.3.60
10	HGF968	11.8.58	54	JXC247		98	JXC291	7.4.60
11	HGF969	22.4.58	55	JXC248	5.1.59	99	JXC292	
12	HGF970	22.4.58	56	JXC249	5.1.59	100	JXC293	
13	HGF971	11.8.58	57	JXC250	11.8.58	101	JXC294	
14	HGF972	11.8.58	58	JXC251	1.8.59	102	JXC295	25.3.60
15	HGF973	11.8.58	59	JXC252	5.1.59	103	JXC296	
16	HGF974	11.8.58	60	JXC253	1.8.59	104	JXC297	
17	HGF975	22.4.58	61	JXC254	1.8.59	105	JXC298	
18	HGF976	11.8.58	62	JXC255	1.8.59	106	JXC299	6.10.62
19	HGF977	22.4.58	63	JXC256	1.8.59	107	JXC300	25.3.60
20	HGF978	22.4.58	64	JXC257	1.8.59	108	JXC301	25.3.60
21	HGF979	22.4.58	65	JXC258	1.8.59	109	JXC302	25.3.60
22	HGF980	22.4.58	66	JXC259	1.8.59	110	JXC303	25.3.60
23	HGF981	22.4.58	67	JXC260	1.8.59	111	JXC304	7.4.60
24	HGF982	22.4.58	68	JXC261	1.8.59	112	JXC305	
25	HGF983	22.4.58	69	JXC262	25.3.60	113	JXC306	7.4.60
26	HGF984	11.8.58	70	JXC263	1.8.59	114	JXC307	
27	HGF985	22.4.58	71	JXC264	1.8.59	115	JXC308	25.3.60
28	HGF986	11.8.58	72	JXC265	1.8.59	116	JXC309	6.10.62
29	HGF987	22.4.58	73	JXC266	1.8.59	117	JXC310	25.3.60
30	HGF988	25.3.60	74	JXC267	6.10.62	118	JXC311	
31	HGF989	22.4.58	75	JXC268	1.8.59	119	JXC312	7.4.60
32	JXC225	1.8.59	76	JXC269	1.8.59	120	JXC313	7.4.60
33	JXC226	1.8.59	77	JXC270	1.8.59	121	JXC314	
34	JXC227	1.8.59	78	JXC271	1.8.59	122	JXC315	25.3.60
35	JXC228	1.8.59	79	JXC272	1.8.59	123	JXC316	6.10.62
36	JXC229	1.8.59	80	JXC273	1.8.59	124	JXC317	
37	JXC230	1.8.59	81	JXC274	1.8.59	125	JXC318	25.3.60
38	JXC231	1.8.59	82	JXC275	1.8.59	126	JXC319	30.8.62
39	JXC232	5.1.59	83	JXC276	1.8.59	127	JXC320	25.3.60
40	JXC233	1.8.59	84	JXC277	1.8.59	128	JXC321	30.8.62
41	JXC234	14.1.59	85	JXC278	1.8.59	129	JXC322	23.5.62
42	JXC235	5.1.59	86	JXC279		130	JXC323	
43	JXC236	1.8.59	87	JXC280	21.6.62	131	JXC324	6.10.62
44	JXC237	5.1.59	88	JXC281	25.3.60			

Leyton's RF 8, carrying a British Railways party to an event at Wembley, was typical of the 1RF1/2 Private Hire coaches after being repainted into this drab all-green livery with red lettering at their first overhaul. R.H.G. Simpson

RF

Replacement of the bulk of London Transport's pre-war single deckers was delayed until the worst of the much larger double-deck fleet had been withdrawn and did not start until 1951. The standard single-decker was to be the AEC Regal IV, a model which was launched by AEC in 1949. Trials carried out by London Transport during 1950 with the demonstrator UMP227 proved successful and an order was placed for 700 chassis with bodywork by Metro-Cammell Carriage & Wagon Co. Ltd. The body-work order was placed in substitution for 550 RTL bodies which were transferred to Park Royal. The standard AEC chassis was modified for London Transport in a number of respects, including the addition of Pilot Injection, a system designed to reduce diesel knock. At the time the orders were placed the regulations restricted the length of single-deckers to twenty-seven feet but the permitted length was increased to thirty feet in 1950. The orders were then altered to a mixture of twenty-seven and thirty footers, as not all routes were then approved for the longer vehicle. Approval was forthcoming later and the order for six hundred and seventy-five was amended to be for thirty-footers. The change in regulations was too late to affect the first twenty-five which were the only production Regal IVs built to the smaller dimensions.

The bodywork for all seven hundred was of basically the same design but there were four major variants. RF 1–25 were the short wheelbase vehicles and were intended for Private Hire and touring work. They had tubular framed seats to Green Line specification, glass observation windows in the side roof panels and public address equipment. RF 26–288 were thirty foot long Green Line coaches with all thirty-nine seats facing forwards; RF 289–513 were forty-one seat Central Area buses and were the only RFs built without platform doors; RF 514–700 were Country Buses, identical to the Central version except for having platform doors. Three of the latter (RFs 517, 647 and 700) were modified for one-man operation before entering service in March 1954 and RF 649 was added in October 1954.

The first Private Hire coaches were licensed in time for the Festival of Britain in May 1951, the Green Line coaches between October 1951 and November 1952, the Central buses between September 1952 and March 1953 and finally the Country buses between March and December 1953. A further seventy-nine were authorised by the British Transport Commission but by 1953 reduced vehicle requirements made this unnecessary and the authority was never taken up.

In 1956, to increase the size of the Green Line fleet, ten of the Private Hire coaches (RF 16–25), six Central Buses (RF 289–294) and nineteen Country Buses (RF 514–516, 697, 518–532, renumbered RF 295–313) were fitted with luggage racks and transferred to Green Line duties. RF 289–294 were also fitted with platform doors and painted green. All the former buses were fitted with saloon heaters and had their seating capacity reduced to forty. As a consequence of these changes, RF 295–313 were renumbered RF 514–532 and RF 517, 647 and 649 renumbered RF 697–699. The loss of six RFs from the Central Bus fleet created a dispute with the staff and was eventually compensated by the transfer of RFs 533–538 to Central Buses at Sidcup garage in December 1956. They remained green until overhauled at the end of 1957, when they also had their platform doors removed.

RF 23 is at Eccleston Bridge Victoria, after being modified for Green Line operation in 1956. A specially modified version of the fixing clips for the side route boards had to be designed to allow for the glass roof panels on these vehicles. G. Mead

RF 282, parked outside Windsor garage, was one of 263 2RF2/1 Green Line coach variants of the Regal IV, which had a livery of two shades of green, side route boards and the Green Line fleetname to distinguish them from others in the class. Alan B. Cross

The 2RF2/2 Country Bus version was in most respects identical to the Central Bus type but was fitted additionally with platform doors and did not have a route plate fixing over the doorway. RF 662 at Dorking shows how the type looked before conversion to one-man operation. Capital Transport Collection

The basic RF design was the 2RF2 Central Bus version which had the same body design as the rest but lacked platform doors, as was still a requirement of the Metropolitan traffic authorities in the 1950s, and was provided with a route number plate fitting above the entrance. RF 386, new in December 1952, is parked at the southern terminus of route 213, 'The California', Belmont. Gerald Mead

RF 505 was one of thirty-seven converted for Central Bus one-man operation in 1959 but not used as such because there was no agreement with the trade union. Instead these 2RF5/3s were used to replace TDs, in this case at Uxbridge. Peter J. Relf

Following the success of the one-man trials in 1954, the Executive authorised further conversions, starting in February 1956 with RFs 682–696 and continuing until all Country Buses had been converted by March 1959. Between March and April 1959 red RFs 502–538 were similarly modified for use on Kingston routes 216, 218 and 219 but agreement with the Trade Union was not forthcoming and the seven vehicles which had been licensed were again delicensed. All thirty-seven re-entered service as two-man buses at Norbiton and Uxbridge in June and Kingston and North Street in July 1959.

In 1956 thirty-eight RFs were fitted experimentally with flashing trafficators similar to those fitted to RMs. They were fitted to all remaining RFs in 1959. The Country Area buses were fitted with saloon heaters between 1961 and 1963.

The 2RF2/2 Country Bus version of the Regal IV had platform doors and did not have a nearside route number plate, but was otherwise identical to the Central Bus type. RF 566 was still being operated as a two-man bus when it was photographed on a Welwyn Garden City new town shortworking of route 372. The bus was modified for one-man operation in March 1959. E.J. Smith

Six green RFs were transferred to Central Buses in December 1956 to restore the number held in the Central Bus fleet. RF 535 is seen at 'The Plough' after having its platform doors removed and being repainted at the beginning of 1958. A.J. Wild

All Country Bus RFs had been modified for one-man operation by March 1959, the main external distinguishing feature being a modified signalling window in three instead of two sections, the 'PAY AS YOU ENTER' transfers on the nearby windscreen being barely visible. RF 659, seen in Gravesend in September 1959, was treated in August 1958.
R.A. Golds

Chassis:	AEC Regal IV 9821LT
Engine:	AEC A219 9.6 litre horizontal 125 bhp
Transmission:	AEC D140 4-speed air operated preselective with fluid flywheel
Bodywork:	Metro-Cammell
Capacity:	DP35F (1–25); DP39F (26–288); B41F (289–516, 518–646, 648–699); B39F OMO (517, 647, 700)
Original L.T. codes:	1RF1/2 (1–25); 2RF2/1 (26–288); 2RF2 (289–513); 2RF2/2 (514–516, 518–646, 648–699); 2RF5 (517, 647, 700)
Built:	1951–1953
Number built:	700
Number in stock:	1.1.55: 700 31.12.62: 700

RF		RF		RF		RF		RF	
1	LUC201	18	LUC218	35	LYF386	52	LYF403	69	LYF420
2	LUC202	19	LUC219	36	LYF387	53	LYF404	70	LYF421
3	LUC203	20	LUC220	37	LYF388	54	LYF405	71	LYF422
4	LUC204	21	LUC221	38	LYF389	55	LYF406	72	LYF423
5	LUC205	22	LUC222	39	LYF390	56	LYF407	73	LYF424
6	LUC206	23	LUC223	40	LYF391	57	LYF408	74	LYF425
7	LUC207	24	LUC224	41	LYF392	58	LYF409	75	LYF426
8	LUC208	25	LUC225	42	LYF393	59	LYF410	76	LYF427
9	LUC209	26	LYF377	43	LYF394	60	LYF411	77	LYF428
10	LUC210	27	LYF378	44	LYF395	61	LYF412	78	LYF429
11	LUC211	28	LYF379	45	LYF396	62	LYF413	79	LYF430
12	LUC212	29	LYF380	46	LYF397	63	LYF414	80	LYF431
13	LUC213	30	LYF381	47	LYF398	64	LYF415	81	LYF432
14	LUC214	31	LYF382	48	LYF399	65	LYF416	82	LYF433
15	LUC215	32	LYF383	49	LYF400	66	LYF417	83	LYF434
16	LUC216	33	LYF384	50	LYF401	67	LYF418	84	LYF435
17	LUC217	34	LYF385	51	LYF402	68	LYF419	85	LYF436

RF		RF		RF		RF		RF	
86	LYF437	154	MLL541	222	MLL609	290	MLL927	358	MLL995
87	LYF438	155	MLL542	223	MLL610	291	MLL928	359	MXX1
88	LYF439	156	MLL543	224	MLL611	292	MLL929	360	MXX2
89	LYF440	157	MLL544	225	MLL612	293	MLL930	361	MXX3
90	LYF441	158	MLL545	226	MLL763	294	MLL931	362	MXX4
91	LYF442	159	MLL546	227	MLL764	* 295	MLL932	363	MXX5
92	LYF443	160	MLL547	228	MLL765	* 296	MLL933	364	MXX6
93	LYF444	161	MLL548	229	MLL766	* 297	MLL934	365	MXX7
94	LYF445	162	MLL549	230	MLL767	* 298	MLL935	366	MXX8
95	LYF446	163	MLL550	231	MLL768	* 299	MLL936	367	MXX9
96	LYF447	164	MLL551	232	MLL769	* 300	MLL937	368	MXX10
97	LYF448	165	MLL552	233	MLL770	* 301	MLL938	369	MXX11
98	LYF449	166	MLL553	234	MLL771	* 302	MLL939	370	MXX12
99	LYF450	167	MLL554	235	MLL772	* 303	MLL940	371	MXX13
100	LYF451	168	MLL555	236	MLL773	* 304	MLL941	372	MXX14
101	LYF452	169	MLL556	237	MLL774	* 305	MLL942	373	MXX15
102	LYF453	170	MLL557	238	MLL775	* 306	MLL943	374	MXX16
103	LYF454	171	MLL558	239	MLL776	* 307	MLL944	375	MXX17
104	LYF455	172	MLL559	240	MLL777	* 308	MLL945	376	MXX18
105	LYF456	173	MLL560	241	MLL778	* 309	MLL946	377	MXX19
106	LYF457	174	MLL561	242	MLL779	* 310	MLL947	378	MXX20
107	LYF458	175	MLL562	243	MLL780	* 311	MLL948	379	MXX21
108	LYF459	176	MLL563	244	MLL781	* 312	MLL949	380	MXX22
109	LYF460	177	MLL564	245	MLL782	* 313	MLL950	381	MXX23
110	LYF461	178	MLL565	246	MLL783	314	MLL951	382	MXX24
111	LYF462	179	MLL566	247	MLL784	315	MLL952	383	MXX25
112	LYF463	180	MLL567	248	MLL785	316	MLL953	384	MXX26
113	LYF464	181	MLL568	249	MLL786	317	MLL954	385	MXX27
114	LYF465	182	MLL569	250	MLL787	318	MLL955	386	MXX28
115	LYF466	183	MLL570	251	MLL788	319	MLL956	387	MXX29
116	LYF467	184	MLL571	252	MLL789	320	MLL957	388	MXX30
117	LYF468	185	MLL572	253	MLL790	321	MLL958	389	MXX277
118	LYF469	186	MLL573	254	MLL791	322	MLL959	390	MXX278
119	LYF470	187	MLL574	255	MLL792	323	MLL960	391	MXX279
120	LYF471	188	MLL575	256	MLL793	324	MLL961	392	MXX280
121	LYF472	189	MLL576	257	MLL794	325	MLL962	393	MXX281
122	LYF473	190	MLL577	258	MLL795	326	MLL963	394	MXX282
123	LYF474	191	MLL578	259	MLL796	327	MLL964	395	MXX283
124	LYF475	192	MLL579	260	MLL797	328	MLL965	396	MXX284
125	LYF476	193	MLL580	261	MLL798	329	MLL966	397	MXX285
126	MLL513	194	MLL581	262	MLL799	330	MLL967	398	MXX286
127	MLL514	195	MLL582	263	MLL800	331	MLL968	399	MXX287
128	MLL515	196	MLL583	264	MLL801	332	MLL969	400	MXX288
129	MLL516	197	MLL584	265	MLL802	333	MLL970	401	MXX289
130	MLL517	198	MLL585	266	MLL803	334	MLL971	402	MXX290
131	MLL518	199	MLL586	267	MLL804	335	MLL972	403	MXX291
132	MLL519	200	MLL587	268	MLL805	336	MLL973	404	MXX292
133	MLL520	201	MLL588	269	MLL806	337	MLL974	405	MXX293
134	MLL521	202	MLL589	270	MLL807	338	MLL975	406	MXX294
135	MLL522	203	MLL590	271	MLL808	339	MLL976	407	MXX295
136	MLL523	204	MLL591	272	MLL809	340	MLL977	408	MXX296
137	MLL524	205	MLL592	273	MLL810	341	MLL978	409	MXX297
138	MLL525	206	MLL593	274	MLL811	342	MLL979	410	MXX298
139	MLL526	207	MLL594	275	MLL812	343	MLL980	411	MXX299
140	MLL527	208	MLL595	276	MLL813	344	MLL981	412	MXX389
141	MLL528	209	MLL596	277	MLL814	345	MLL982	413	MXX390
142	MLL529	210	MLL597	278	MLL815	346	MLL983	414	MXX391
143	MLL530	211	MLL598	279	MLL816	347	MLL984	415	MXX392
144	MLL531	212	MLL599	280	MLL817	348	MLL985	416	MXX393
145	MLL532	213	MLL600	281	MLL818	349	MLL986	417	MXX394
146	MLL533	214	MLL601	282	MLL819	350	MLL987	418	MXX395
147	MLL534	215	MLL602	283	MLL820	351	MLL988	419	MXX396
148	MLL535	216	MLL603	284	MLL821	352	MLL989	420	MXX397
149	MLL536	217	MLL604	285	MLL822	353	MLL990	421	MXX398
150	MLL537	218	MLL605	286	MLL823	354	MLL991	422	MXX399
151	MLL538	219	MLL606	287	MLL824	355	MLL992	423	MXX400
152	MLL539	220	MLL607	288	MLL825	356	MLL993	424	MXX401
153	MLL540	221	MLL608	289	MLL926	357	MLL994	425	MXX402

* Renumbered in 1956 – see list on page 101.

RF

RF		RF		RF		RF		RF	
426	MXX403	481	MXX458	536	NLE536	591	NLE591	646	NLE646
427	MXX404	482	MXX459	537	NLE537	592	NLE592	* 647	NLE647
428	MXX405	483	MXX460	538	NLE538	593	NLE593	648	NLE648
429	MXX406	484	MXX461	539	NLE539	594	NLE594	* 649	NLE649
430	MXX407	485	MXX462	540	NLE540	595	NLE595	650	NLE650
431	MXX408	486	MXX463	541	NLE541	596	NLE596	651	NLE651
432	MXX409	487	MXX464	542	NLE542	597	NLE597	652	NLE652
433	MXX410	488	MXX465	543	NLE543	598	NLE598	653	NLE653
434	MXX411	489	MXX466	544	NLE544	599	NLE599	654	NLE654
435	MXX412	490	MXX467	545	NLE545	600	NLE600	655	NLE655
436	MXX413	491	MXX468	546	NLE546	601	NLE601	656	NLE656
437	MXX414	492	MXX469	547	NLE547	602	NLE602	657	NLE657
438	MXX415	493	MXX470	548	NLE548	603	NLE603	658	NLE658
439	MXX416	494	MXX471	549	NLE549	604	NLE604	659	NLE659
440	MXX417	495	MXX472	550	NLE550	605	NLE605	660	NLE660
441	MXX418	496	MXX473	551	NLE551	606	NLE606	661	NLE661
442	MXX419	497	MXX474	552	NLE552	607	NLE607	662	NLE662
443	MXX420	498	MXX475	553	NLE553	608	NLE608	663	NLE663
444	MXX421	499	MXX476	554	NLE554	609	NLE609	664	NLE664
445	MXX422	500	MXX477	555	NLE555	610	NLE610	665	NLE665
446	MXX423	501	MXX478	556	NLE556	611	NLE611	666	NLE666
447	MXX424	502	MXX479	557	NLE557	612	NLE612	667	NLE667
448	MXX425	503	MXX480	558	NLE558	613	NLE613	668	NLE668
449	MXX426	504	MXX481	559	NLE559	614	NLE614	669	NLE669
450	MXX427	505	MXX482	560	NLE560	615	NLE615	670	NLE670
451	MXX428	506	MXX483	561	NLE561	616	NLE616	671	NLE671
452	MXX429	507	MXX484	562	NLE562	617	NLE617	672	NLE672
453	MXX430	508	MXX485	563	NLE563	618	NLE618	673	NLE673
454	MXX431	509	MXX486	564	NLE564	619	NLE619	674	NLE674
455	MXX432	510	MXX487	565	NLE565	620	NLE620	675	NLE675
456	MXX433	511	MXX488	566	NLE566	621	NLE621	676	NLE676
457	MXX434	512	MXX489	567	NLE567	622	NLE622	677	NLE677
458	MXX435	513	MXX490	568	NLE568	623	NLE623	678	NLE678
459	MXX436	* 514	NLE514	569	NLE569	624	NLE624	679	NLE679
460	MXX437	* 515	NLE515	570	NLE570	625	NLE625	680	NLE680
461	MXX438	* 516	NLE516	571	NLE571	626	NLE626	681	NLE681
462	MXX439	* 517	NLE517	572	NLE572	627	NLE627	682	NLE682
463	MXX440	* 518	NLE518	573	NLE573	628	NLE628	683	NLE683
464	MXX441	* 519	NLE519	574	NLE574	629	NLE629	684	NLE684
465	MXX442	* 520	NLE520	575	NLE575	630	NLE630	685	NLE685
466	MXX443	* 521	NLE521	576	NLE576	631	NLE631	686	NLE686
467	MXX444	* 522	NLE522	577	NLE577	632	NLE632	687	NLE687
468	MXX445	* 523	NLE523	578	NLE578	633	NLE633	688	NLE688
469	MXX446	* 524	NLE524	579	NLE579	634	NLE634	689	NLE689
470	MXX447	* 525	NLE525	580	NLE580	635	NLE635	690	NLE690
471	MXX448	* 526	NLE526	581	NLE581	636	NLE636	691	NLE691
472	MXX449	* 527	NLE527	582	NLE582	637	NLE637	692	NLE692
473	MXX450	* 528	NLE528	583	NLE583	638	NLE638	693	NLE693
474	MXX451	* 529	NLE529	584	NLE584	639	NLE639	694	NLE694
475	MXX452	* 530	NLE530	585	NLE585	640	NLE640	695	NLE695
476	MXX453	* 531	NLE531	586	NLE586	641	NLE641	696	NLE696
477	MXX454	* 532	NLE532	587	NLE587	642	NLE642	697	NLE697
478	MXX455	533	NLE533	588	NLE588	643	NLE643	* 698	NLE698
479	MXX456	534	NLE534	589	NLE589	644	NLE644	* 699	NLE699
480	MXX457	535	NLE535	590	NLE590	645	NLE645	700	NLE700

* These buses were renumbered in 1956, exchanging numbers as follows:

295/514	23.3.56	303/522	19.3.56	310/529	9.3.56
296/515	22.3.56	304/523	16.3.56	311/530	5.4.56
297/516	4.4.56	305/524	16.4.56	312/531	9.3.56
299/518	22.3.56	306/525	28.3.56	313/532	23.4.56
300/519	11.4.56	307/526	18.4.56	647/698	26.1.56
301/520	11.4.56	308/527	28.3.56	649/699	26.1.56
302/521	12.4.56	309/528	29.3.56		

RF 298 was renumbered RF 517; RF 517 renumbered RF 697; RF 697 renumbered RF 298 on 28.3.56

This group of GSs is at the hub of a small local network of 'small saloon OMO' routes, Rickmansworth Car Park. The special design of twenty-six seat body produced by Eastern Coach Works was happily at home in the London Transport post-war family but was the first standard London design to have sliding vent windows. R.H.G. Simpson

GS

To replace its fleet of small twenty-seat Leyland Cub one-man buses London Transport chose a modified version of the Guy Vixen chassis incorporating some Otter parts and a special bonnet made by Briggs Motor Bodies of Dagenham. The Perkins oil engine was specified and transmission was through a normal clutch and crash gearbox. The Eastern Coach Works bodies were built to a design which had many characteristics of contemporary LT practice but with standard ECW internal finishings. The seating capacity of twenty-six took advantage of new regulations which allowed one-man operation of buses up to that capacity. The first GSs went into service at Chelsham in October 1953 and the remainder were allocated in small numbers all around the fleet. Introduction of one-man operation with RFs and the general contraction of services weakened the role of the twenty-six seaters and withdrawal of the class began as early as January 1961. They were fitted with flashing trafficators in 1959/1960.

Chassis:	Guy Vixen	
Engine:	Perkins P6 indirect-injection 65 bhp	
Transmission:	4-speed crash	
Bodywork:	Eastern Coach Works	
Capacity:	B26F	
L.T. code:	1GS1	
Built:	1953	
Number built:	84	
Number in stock: 1.1.55: 84		31.12.62: 74

The offside of the GS was a happy blend of its varied elements into a coherent and well balanced design, the potentially awkward transition from main body to the bonnet and wing area being particularly elegantly achieved. GS 19 is at Hertford bus station on a Saturday short to Bulls Green in August 1955. W.R. Legg

GS		Date out of stock	GS		Date out of stock	GS		Date out of stock
1	MXX301		29	MXX329		57	MXX357	
2	MXX302		30	MXX330		58	MXX358	
3	MXX303		31	MXX331		59	MXX359	
4	MXX304		32	MXX332	12.6.61	60	MXX360	
5	MXX305		33	MXX333		61	MXX361	17.4.61
6	MXX306		34	MXX334		62	MXX362	
7	MXX307		35	MXX335		63	MXX363	8.5.61
8	MXX308		36	MXX336		64	MXX364	
9	MXX309		37	MXX337	13.6.61	65	MXX365	
10	MXX310		38	MXX338		66	MXX366	
11	MXX311		39	MXX339		67	MXX367	
12	MXX312		40	MXX340	16.1.61	68	MXX368	
13	MXX313		41	MXX341	16.1.61	69	MXX369	
14	MXX314		42	MXX342		70	MXX370	26.4.61
15	MXX315		43	MXX343	24.5.61	71	MXX371	
16	MXX316		44	MXX344		72	MXX372	
17	MXX317		45	MXX345		73	MXX373	
18	MXX318		46	MXX346		74	MXX374	
19	MXX319		47	MXX347		75	MXX375	
20	MXX320		48	MXX348		76	MXX376	
21	MXX321		49	MXX349	24.5.61	77	MXX377	
22	MXX322		50	MXX350		78	MXX378	
23	MXX323		51	MXX351		79	MXX379	
24	MXX324	8.6.61	52	MXX352		80	MXX380	
25	MXX325		53	MXX353		81	MXX381	
26	MXX326		54	MXX354		82	MXX382	
27	MXX327		55	MXX355		83	MXX383	
28	MXX328		56	MXX356		84	MXX384	

The very distinctive lines of their ECW bodywork and their handsome green and grey colour scheme made the RFWs stand out from the highly standardised crowd in London Transport's fleet. RFW 2 is at Tower Hill on the City of London tour, one of the tasks found for them after their original function of operating on long distance contract carriage work was abolished by the Conservative government in 1953. Alan B. Cross

RFW

In May 1950 the British Transport Commission gave London Transport authority to operate contract carriage services up to a one hundred mile radius from 55 Broadway, for which purpose the Executive purchased fifteen luxury coaches, five of which had been diverted by the BTC from a Tilling group company. The chassis was the eight foot wide version of the Regal IV built to the newly authorised length of thirty-feet. They were standard 9821E models but with some modifications for London Transport. The thirty-nine seat bodies supplied by Eastern Coach Works were of a rather austere design but interior furnishings and fittings were to full coach standards. They had glass observation panels at cant level, swing passenger door and no destination indicators. All fifteen entered service in May and June 1951 and were allocated to both Central and Country garages. They were fitted with flashing trafficators in 1959/1960.

Chassis:	AEC Regal IV 9821E
Engine:	AEC A219 9.6 litre horizontal 125 bhp
Transmission:	AEC D140 4-speed air operated preselective with fluid flywheel
Bodywork:	Eastern Coach Works
Capacity:	C39F
L.T. code:	3RF3
Built:	1951
Number built:	15
Number in stock:	1.1.55: 15 31.12.62: 15

RFW

1	LUC376
2	LUC377
3	LUC378
4	LUC379
5	LUC380

RFW

6	LUC381
7	LUC382
8	LUC283
9	LUC384
10	LUC385

RFW

11	LUC386
12	LUC387
13	LUC388
14	LUC389
15	LUC390

The three Willowbrook bodied AEC Reliances which formed the RW class were identical to a batch supplied to Grimsby-Cleethorpes Transport and had few standard London Transport features, confined to elements of the interior trim. The purpose of their experimental operation was to try out a two-door arrangement, with a separate centre exit. RW 2 is seen at Warners End on its first Sunday of operation. Ken Glazier

RW

After six years' experience of one-man operation using the RF, which had not been designed for this function, London Transport wished to find ways of reducing the time spent at stops. For this purpose, three Willowbrook bodied AEC Reliances with separate front entrance and centre exit were purchased in 1960. To secure quick delivery they were identical to a batch designed for standee operation, then being built for Grimsby-Cleethorpes Transport, to whose production run they were added. Apart from the door arrangements, the RWs were unusual in having quarter light windows in the cant panels, three on the nearside and five offside. The interior finish was as specified by Grimsby-Cleethorpes but with some standard London Transport trim. RW 1–3 entered service on the busy route 322 from Two Waters garage on 26th September 1960 and later ran from St Albans (355), Hertford (333/333B) and Addlestone (427/437/456). They were withdrawn from service in October 1963 and sold to Chesterfield Corporation.

Chassis:	AEC Reliance 2MU2RA
Engine:	AEC AH470 7.7 litre horizontal 100 bhp
Transmission:	AEC D182 Monocontrol 4-speed direct acting electro-pneumatic with fluid flywheel.
Bodywork:	Willowbrook
Capacity:	B42D
L.T. code:	1RW1
Built:	1960
Number built:	3

RW		Date into stock	RW		Date into stock	RW		Date into stock
1	495ALH	30.8.60	2	496ALH	1.9.60	3	497ALH	15.9.60

APPENDIX: THE 1958 BUS STRIKE

The People's League for the Defence of Freedom

This right-wing political organisation operated buses on up to seven routes during the strike of London busmen, starting on 31st May carrying passengers free. Exceptionally, London Transport granted Consents for these routes and by 13th June, the League was able to charge fares. Twenty buses were bought or borrowed from a dealer and were operated from Kendals car park on the north side of Wandsworth Common. Although these buses were never owned by London Transport and, apart from the technicality of Consent, were not under London Transport's control, the event was of such importance that a list (courtesy of the PSV Circle) of those vehicles known to have been operated and a selection of photographs is considered appropriate.

List of buses operated by the People's League for the Defence of Freedom

(Vehicles run by other organisations were usually hired from existing operators)

				Former Owner
FT5702	AEC Regent 0661	Weymann	H56R	Tynemouth & District
JG9934	Leyland Tiger TS8	Park Royal	C32R	East Kent Road Car
JG9956	Leyland Tiger TS8	Park Royal	C32R	East Kent Road Car
ABE335	Leyland Tiger TS8	Harrington	C34F	Lincolnshire Road Car
BFN934	Leyland Titan TD7	Park Royal	H53R	Crosville MS
BFN939	Leyland Titan TD7	Park Royal	H53R	Crosville MS
BTF21	Leyland Tiger LT7C	Leyland	B34R	Lytham St Annes Corporation
BTF28	Leyland Titan TD4C	Leyland	FH54R	Lytham St Annes Corporation
CFM361	Leyland Titan TD5	ECW	L55R	Crosville MS
CFM365	Leyland Titan TD5	ECW	L55R	Crosville MS
CRX540	Bristol K6A	Strachan	L55R	Thames Valley Traction
DBC221	AEC Renown 0664	Met-Camm	H64R	Leicester Corporation
DBC224	AEC Renown 0664	Met-Camm	H64R	Leicester Corporation
DLY984	Dennis Lancet II	Duple	C35F	Empress, London E2
DUC904	Leyland Tiger TS7D	Beadle	B43C	City Coach Co.
EWO475	Bedford OWB	?	?	Red & White MS
FTD618	Daimler CWA6	Duple	H56R	Lytham St Annes Corporation
GCD688	Leyland Titan TD7	Park Royal	H52R	Crosville MS
HTC614	Crossley SD42	Crossley	B36R	Leicester Corporation
HTC615	Crossley SD42	Crossley	B36R	Leicester Corporation

Nearly half the vehicles used were single-deck, including some coaches. Former Lytham St Annes Corporation Leyland LT7C, Leyland bodied, was photographed in Brixton on route 6 (Oval–Thornton Heath). A.B. Cross

BFN934, a former Crosville Motor Services Park Royal bodied Leyland Tian TD7, is at Marble Arch on route '1'.
Capital Transport Collection

Pre-war AEC Regent FT5702, a former Tynemouth vehicle, was used to advertise the purpose of the demonstration.
Capital Transport Collection

Another former Crosville bus was CFM365, a Leyland TD5 with ECW lowbridge bodywork. It is seen at the outer end of route 6 (Oval–Thornton Heath). D.A. Ruddom Collection

This oddity was not operated by the League but by a West End car dealer. It was a scooter and bubble car transporter mounted on a former Aldershot & District Dennis Lancet chassis. Capital Transport Collection

The Aftermath of the 1958 Bus Strike

After a seven week complete close down of bus services in May and June 1958, London Transport suffered a serious loss of passenger traffic and instituted heavy cuts to reduce service levels in response. The first round, on 20th August 1958, saw the complete withdrawal of twenty Central Area bus routes, a few examples of this are illustrated here.

Route 58 was a poorly used suburban service, whose importance had been undermined eighteen years earlier when route 102 was diverted through Hampstead Garden Suburb to Golders Green. The remaining links unique to the 58 were not well used but were partly covered by the diversion of route 143 via The Bishops Avenue. Holloway's (J) RT 751 was photographed on the Archway stand in Brookside Road on 2nd August 1958. R.A. Golds

Once a major north–south trunk route across London, by 1958 the 67 was relatively short and heavily paralleled. Its only section of solo running was in Chancery Lane, where RTL 473 was photographed.
C. Carter

Route 96 was a long-standing operation which was axed because it not only ran through the same corridor as the District Line but also paralleled other bus routes over long stretches of road. Metro-Cammell bodied RTL 957 is seen at the north end of Putney Bridge, its blind already changed for its return journey, a Saturday working to Aldwych. A.M. Wright

Peak hour only route 149 had started only in January 1952 as a replacement for tram route 52 but did not survive the 1958 cuts. RT 522, a 3RT3, is on the Cannon Street station stand in Dowgate Hill. D.A. Ruddom Collection

The withdrawal of route 238, on which RT 957 is operating, left Parkstone Avenue, Emerson Park, without a service for a time. A.M. Wright

Route 251A had started life as a replacement for the peak hour extension of route 2 to Arnos Grove in 1946 and was another 1958 casualty. RT 3584 is in Oakleigh Road. Don Thompson

Route 127 was another suburban route covered entirely by other services, except for two unique 'round-the-corner' links. RLH 63 is seen at Raynes Park station on the last day, 19th August 1958. The displaced RLHs were later used to replace RFs on route 208A, which was renumbered 178. A.B. Cross

One of the Country Bus casualties was route 400, an experimental service linking New Addington, where GS 38 was photographed, with Warlingham Park Hospital. It had the bad luck to be scheduled to start with the summer programme on 18th May 1958 and survived its belated introduction on 22nd June only until 29th October. Ron Wellings